Reset Your Mindset for *Success*.

DINGAAN RAHLAPANE

Reset Your Mindset for Success.

Amazing powers for mindset change

answers consultation Publishers

First published by Answers Consultation, 2021

RESET YOUR MINDSET FOR SUCCESS

Copyright © 2021 by Dingaan Rahlapane

All rights reserved. No part of this text may be reproduced, transmitted, decompiled, reverse engineered or stored in a retrieval system, in any form or by any means, whether electronic or mechanical, now known or hereinafter invented, without the express written permission of Dingaan Rahlapane and the publisher.

Cover Design by: Answers Consultation | Karabo Lekalakala
Edited & Proofread by: Linda F. Mabaso *(Editor)*
Typesetting by: Karabo Lekalakala

Answers Consultation Publishers
27 Matt Street,
Mooikloof Gardens
Pretoria East
0184
www.answersconsultation.com
info@answersconsultation.com
Tel: 087 379 5049
Fax: 086 435 8123

ISBN: 978-0-639-90151-0

A legal deposit of this book is available at, **National Library of South Africa** under Legal Deposit Act, no. 54 of 1997

National Library of South Africa: Pretoria Campus
228 Johannes Ramokhoase St,
Pretoria Central
Pretoria,
0002
www.nlsa.ac.za
Tel: 012 401 9700
Fax: 012 325 5984
Email: infodesk@nlsa.ac.za

Private Bag X990
Pretoria
0001
South Africa

We hope you enjoy the wisdom in this book by Dingaan. Our goal and aim is to publish thought-provoking books that will transform people's lives for the better through wisdom, knowledge and a greater understanding of modern-day society.

Acknowledgements

Firstly, a big thank you to my Creator, the Lord Jesus Christ for the gift I have and the desire I received to undertake this all-important task.

It is often said that individuals alone never accomplished great inventions in solitude. The same is true considering the journey I embarked on to have this project become a reality.

I wish to express my deepest appreciation to my beautiful and supportive wife, Mmathabo Rahlapane. Your sincere support, encouragement and unwavering belief that this could be possible has me in awe. To my children, my three wonderful blessings, Karabo, Orefile and Rethabile. I appreciate the interest you have each shown in this work and your willingness to follow suit in future. With you as my family, I know I have a winning team.

My extended gratitude to the editorial team of Answers Consultation for their diligent work in the editing and proofreading of this book to ensure that it took the right shape.

Lastly, I express my humble gratitude to you, the reader for choosing the book and seeking knowledge into becoming a better version of yourself.

CONTENTS

1. Live the Life of Your Dreams – Find Your Purpose……………………………1
2. Identify and Share Your Gifts...…………11
3. Find Your Vision and Follow It……………17
4. Set Meaningful Goals………..…………….25
5. Secret Knowledge of Power…………....…...33
6. The Power of Your Subconscious Mind…......39
7. Change Your Thoughts, Change Your Life...51
8. Let Go of Your Fears……………………....…..67
9. Create Your Reality through Imagination…..73
10. Reprogramme Your Mind - Auto Hypnosis..77
11. Visualisation and Meditation………………81
12. Supercharge your Brain: Affirmations and Incantations……………………………...97
13. Have an Attitude of Gratitude……………103
14. Press On, Never Give Up – Persistence and Perserverance………………………..107
15. Author's notes & instructions…………….115
16. Suggested Readings………………………121
17. About The Author………………………123
18. Copyrights………………………………..125

Preface

There are obviously a countless number of books in the market and each serving a specific purpose to its reader. The purpose is penetrated through the readers' interests in either comic, religion, fiction, leadership, financial, psychological, or self-help etc. This book in particular, is a self-help book aimed at helping unleash the potential latent within you.

As a Life Coach, I am always excited when I witness people realizing their potential power. However, it also pains just as much to see that there are so many people going through life with so much lack. It is as though the world has run out of resources for their supply.

Perhaps you have read many self-help books, or watched a few Youtube videos or listened to a few podcasts and attend excellent seminars. If you have, then you know that if you do not practice what you have learned, all the learning becomes futile. It is my greatest desire that once you have gone through the entire book, the person who began paging through the first chapter and the one to close the last page will not be the same. I hope a new world would have opened before your eyes and a new reality experienced or awaits to be experienced. Therefore, it is important to know that you can only maximise the beneficial takeaways from this book by practicing the suggestions and techniques indicated.

Chapter One

Live the Life of Your Dreams – Find Your Purpose

"True desire in the heart for anything good is God's proof to you, set beforehand, that it is yours already." - Denzel Washington

If you could do one thing to transform your life, I would highly recommend it to be that you find something you are passionate about and make a living out of it. Learning how to find your passion may not be as easy as it sounds but it is well worth the effort. Throughout my life, I have come to notice that whenever people make or create things, there is a particular reason for the creation.

All products are deemed successful only when they perform the work they were intended to do by the manufacturer. Likewise, a project is a success only if it does or performs the functions for which it was intended for. Hence, there is a reason for every creation, which ultimately serves a purpose. "Many are the plans in a man's heart, but it is the LORD's purpose that will prevail," Proverbs 19:21. You must believe in a course bigger than yourself, a calling for your existence.

Discovering your purpose includes answering questions like, "what is the meaning of life?" or "what is life all about?" and "why am I here?"

Living within your purpose means living with intention and enjoying each day of your life instead of feeling miserable when you face certain days, especially Mondays while being happy on other days, which are mostly weekends. Where purpose is not known, abuse is inevitable meaning that if you do not know the purpose of something you are likely to abuse it. A kitchen knife cannot be used to cut a tree because it was not meant (purposed) cut down trees. Your task is to make sure that you do not abuse your life by not living within your purpose.

Much as it is important to live within your purpose there are however, still so many people who are living without a purpose and some of the reasons why that is so include the following:

- **Not enough investment in self-growth** - Some of the questions to ask yourself with regards to living a purposeful life are; how much time do I spend working on myself? How much time do I spend every day working on my dreams? In the last ninety days, how many books have I read? In the last year how many skills or knowledge did I aquire? What kind of investment have I made on myself? To really live the life of your dreams you have to make a conscious effort to begin working on yourself.
- **Seeking perfect conditions** - Some people's desire include not making mistakes, to be liked by others and to be perfect each time they do something. The reality is that you are going to make mistakes along the way. You may hurt some people's feelings (mostly those enjoying the comfort zone), and you may even make enemies in the process. Either way, you must not allow the desire for perfection to hold you back from living your dreams.

- **Self-doubt** - Other people do not live their dreams because they are governed by their old disempowering habits, including their fears and opinions of others. Many people have never tried anything different because the people that they value managed to convince them of how they cannot do it. They are living in the context that other people have of them, which mostly encompasses of low expectations. While others doubt themselves because when they wanted to do something in the past someone they love or someone they respected said, "No, you can't do that" and they believed them. Instead of wallowing in despair, choose to ask yourself certain empowering questions like; "What would my life be like if I decided not to listen to my fears? What would my life be like if I did not care what people thought about me? Or what would my life be like if I decided to be courageous instead of giving into what others think or say about me?"
- Fears of the unknown and pain of change - Most people are not living their dreams because of the fear of the unknown. They do not want to move from their comfort zones nor do they want to let go of the familiar, as they are likely to feel vulnerable in new spaces. Be encouraged to rather not wait for things to be perfect or to have the ideal situation at hand in order to start living your dreams. The untold truth is, things will never be perfect and if that is what you seek, then you are most likely not going to start. You must do what you can with what you currently have and live by faith. *"Faith is like a muscle. It only grows through repeated use."* - Joyce Meyer

- **Avoiding being hurt** - The other reason is that some people do not want to feel the pain that comes with change but unfortunately, as you live you will realise that it is difficult to avoid it because pain is everywhere. No matter where you hide, pain is there, it is inevitable. People fear many things, it can either be the pain of defeat, the pain of disappointment, the pain of losing, the pain of failure, the pain of not being liked by others, and to some extent the pain of being criticised, etc. The reality is, pain is everywhere, and you cannot duck nor hide from it. It is often said that there is no gain without pain. Victor Frankl calls it unavoidable suffering; it is everywhere. Nevertheless, I guess it would be better to deal with pain while you are building a legacy for your life than toiling for other people.
- **Not good enough and not worth it** - Perhaps you are among those who may have not been discouraged by others or even afraid of the unknown. However, you happen to be part of those who feel that they do not have what it takes to live the lives they have dreamt of. You probably do not feel like life is worth chasing after dreams nor is it worth nurturing your gift/s. You may also tend to feel that you do not have the necessary connections and resources that it will take for you to live up to your dreams. If that is you, then I urge you to not allow that inner self-doubt to talk you out of it. Do not let it tell you why you are not good enough and build a case on why you cannot do it. Ignore that negative inner voice and all other external voices from the naysayers. Do not determine what you can do based on your

resources. Do not determine your possibilities based on your circumstances, for those circumstances will not determine who you are. Your possibilities are unlimited. Even if you are coming back from adversity and devastation, the possibilities are still unlimited. This is the type of capacity human beings possess. In fact, it does not matter how many mistakes you have made in the past or how much money you have lost nor how many flops you have had. These will only add as investments of what is possible for you.

- **Fear of failure** - One of the things many people get scared of are the endless possibilities of failure. What I often tell people is that success will come with its own failures. As harsh as this may sound but you will fail your way to success. It has been said that 8 out of 10 millionaires were once bankrupt. Therefore, contrary to what society has told you there is nothing wrong with failing. Failure is simply a lesson learned. You are only considered a true failure if you do not learn the lesson brought by failure. It has been stated that Thomas Edison failed 1 000 times before he could perfect his invention of the electric light bulb. When Arnold Schwarzenegger was once asked about failure he said, "Hey we all fail but you are only considered a loser if you fall and never get up. Winners fail and get up all the time and that is the spirit of the winner". Therefore, do not worry if you fail even if it happens more often than you had expected.

Knowing what you want in this life should be at the core of our very existence. That reminds me of one of Oprah Winfrey's interview with the host of The Daily Show, Trevor Noah. In that interview, only one question stood out that required her to name the one common characteristic that gets people to where they want to be in life. Oprah responded by saying, "People get successful in life because they know where they want to go. Many people are driven by what they think they should do or what others say they should do but the most important question to ask yourself is "what do I really want?"

History records are filled with biographies about people who not only lived a purposeful life but also exercised their gifts with precision. Some of these examples are icons like Nelson Mandela, whose endeavor to bring freedom for black people and create a democratic South Africa was an embodiment of his purpose. His incredible negotiation skills, peace-making tactics and reconciliation are very much notable. Martin Luther King Jnr is also an icon of note. He fought for equality and human rights for African Americans by vigorously using his gifts as an orator and motivator. You may be thinking of a few others who not only discovered their purpose and gifts but put it all too good use. In emphasizing the importance of a purpose and gifts, you need to follow your heart and search for meaning. Your purpose can make your current job feel frustrating and very unfulfilling at times.

Follow your heart - It is my humble belief that all of us were born to be known for something and that something will only be achieved if we dare to follow our dreams and exercise our gifts. We all have that small voice within us that keeps telling us that certain things should be done differently. The very same voice that makes us slightly angry when we see things not done the way we feel or think they ought to be done. The persistence in that voice is a sure sign that you need to follow your heart and live the life of your dreams. The voice I am talking about here is your intuition, an idea that keeps coming back to you repeatedly. Once you listen to this inner voice and actually begin to act on your dream by doing what you can with what you have, you will notice that things will actually start happening for you. Ideas will come out of nowhere, people will come to you because that which you give our energy and focus to, is returned and will begin to multiply, and expand because where your focus goes, energy flows. Out of that then comes your greatness and the powers within are unleashed. Unfortunately, the powers that we have will not reveal themselves if you do not challenge them.

Search for meaning - In the book, Man's Search for Meaning, by Victor E. Frankl, a holocaust survivor. He stated the following in describing his experience regarding the state of mind of those captured. "The prisoner who had lost faith in the future -his future- was doomed. With his loss of belief in the future, he also lost his spiritual hold; he let himself decline and became subject to mental and physical decay". To survive in those camps, he emphasised on the importance of a change of mind or approach in life. "Men needed a fundamental change in attitude towards life and that it did not really matter what we expected from life but rather what life expected from us. Men needed to stop asking about the meaning of life but instead to think of them as being questioned about life - daily and hourly".

"They who have no central purpose in their life fall an easy prey to worries, troubles, fears and self-pitying, all of which lead to failures, unhappiness and weakness." - James Allen

How to discover your purpose – Here are a few steps that you can apply:

- **Diving In/Introspection** - You need to ask yourself questions such as "what are the things I love the most, what are the things am I interested in?" and the constant seeking of an answer to these questions can reveal your purpose. Your purpose will always provide a bit of clues in your life, as it is a part of who you are.
- **Journaling** - Writing down your thoughts or ideas in a journal, which does not have to be fancy. You can purchase one from any stationary store. However, in order for the process to begin, all you need to have are two things. Firstly, you need to either have a pen or pencil and secondly a journal. Once you have these two items you now good to go! From there on pen down everything and write as much as you can. Do not stop writing, but rather keep the pen moving because the more you write, the more ideas will flow from you. When you have written as much as you can, you will begin to notice a pattern on the ideas you are getting and this will give you enough signage of your purpose. Once you are done writing the notes, your next step is to structure the words into simple sentences that convey strong feelings for you. After that, you must reduce all your sentences into one sentence, which according to you best represents your entire life purpose. This will then be the statement you will display at all places as a reminder to yourself and serve as a source of self-encouragement.

- **Meditation** - Meditation is simply the practice of being still, paying attention to the body, and focusing on your breathing (taking longer, slower and deeper breaths). Through meditation, the true purpose of life can become clear but only for the true seeker, one who truly desires to know, the one who is earnest, undistracted and unafraid. In his 1 000 participant's decade-long series of experiments, Dr Daryl Bem, Cornell University's physicist turned psychologist discovered that humans do indeed have the ability to sense the future. It is one of the best techniques for receiving intuitive and messages that encourage creativity from the inner powers to reveal your life purpose. Meditation will be discussed in detail later in this book.
- **Listen to feedback from people around you** - You may find valuable insight from people around you most of the time. The people you know may at times be able to tell you about things you do effortlessly without even noticing it. This may include family, friends, colleagues etc. Ask them about what comes into their minds every time they think of your name. There is also a good chance that you are already displaying your passion and purpose to those around you without even realizing it. One way you might notice this is, when someone gives you a compliment after certain interactions.
- **Take risks: Try new things** - In order to find or discover your gift you need to listen to your heart and try out new things, which may include things that you may have been afraid to do. By not exposing yourself to

new things, you can never truly know what you really like or are good at. Break free from the usual routines you have grown accustomed too. Take the initiative to jump at the opportunity of new things. Do not worry if you do not know these new things, you will learn along the way. Just remember that all great things come from taking risks. The main point here is that in order to discover your gift, you are going to have to step outside your comfort zone.

- **Consider injustices in the world** - The other best way to identify your purpose is to check things you consider as injustices in the world. These are things you strongly feel something must be done about them but for some reason you feel they are not getting enough attention. This might be a sign that you are supposed to come and solve those particular concerns.
- **Benefits for living your dreams** - There can be no doubt that the people living the lives of their dreams experience much more fulfilling lives than those who don't. Some of the benefits of living a life of purpose is that it gives hope, a sense of contribution, success and fulfillment. Once you have discovered your purpose, you can then start to.

Chapter Two
Identify And Share Your Gifts

"God never put a soul on earth without endowing it with a gift."
- Steve Harvey

Once you are clear about your purpose you can then use the following guide to identify the types of gifts you have in order to accomplish your purpose. Most of the time whenever the subject of gifts comes up people think of gifted people within the entertainment field but the reality is that gifts are much more than that. We all came here on earth bearing gifts. A gift is something given willingly to someone without payment, it is a present or natural ability or talent. Remember that your purpose defines your gift while it takes a gift to fulfil a purpose. Your gift is the source of your value and a source of your wealth.

Proverbs 18:16, "A man's gift makes room for him and brings him before the great."

The two ways you may use to identify a gift:

- **Effortlessness** – One of the best ways to identify your gift is to check the things that you do so well and with the least amount of effort. You do this and it feels so easy for you that you even get surprised when people congratulate or thank you for it. That is certainly a sign of how you were naturally wired to excel in that gift.
- Anger or frustration – The other way to identify your gift is by taking note of the things that evoke the feelings

of sadness or anger when they are not done to your satisfactory. These things get you frustrated because you feel they must be done in a certain way that is better than the one initially used. Once you have identified your gift, it is then time to make sure that you develop it.

Below are few ways that can greatly help you with developing your gift and these are:

- **Study and invest in your gift** - You need to refine and mold your gift by studying everything and anything there is to learn in your field. Read books, and watch YouTube videos if need be and model people you know who have excelled in the same field. The world is changing at an alarming rate and it will be beneficial for you to always keep track of the latest developments in your chosen field. If possible, make sure that learning something new in that particular field is at the top of your list. Invest time into developing or shaping your gift and each time you do that, give it all that you possibly can to make it work.

- **Associate with the right people and eliminate negative influence** - There are certain people in this world who are simply negative about anything and everything they encounter. For them life is all about complaints about greed, corruption, and the lack of opportunities and while it is important to listen to people's views on life, sometimes it is extremely hard to keep your head up when you are surrounded by people who bring you down. You need people around you who are doing well and have a positive outlook about life. The important thing to do is to associate yourself with people in your chosen gifting. Stick with winners in order to become one of them. You need to be able to identify the negative people in your life and get rid of them once and for all.

- **Exercise and volunteer your gift** - If you do not exercise your gift unfortunately, it will not be refined. Volunteer to do any work in your chosen field. Be willing to make mistakes as you go along and remember that anything worth doing is worth doing wrong until you get it right. Commit to taking on any opportunity even if it means failing. However, note that failing is but a natural part of success. In fact, disappointment and embarrassments should help propel you to greater heights instead of slowing you down. Therefore, do not take them personally. Instead, you will find yourself using such defining moments in future to motivate other people who are in similar situations that you were once in. Whenever possible take on something or tasks that frighten you but where you know that you are bound to learn something. The more you do these assignments or practices, the better you become at them and the better refined your gist will be.

In as much as it is critical to identify your gifts, it is also quite important that you develop ways of protecting and nurturing them. This is simply because the world is full of gifted people who fell prey to failure that came with sustaining their gift and they let everything come crumbling down to the delight of their enemies. You may want to come back to this section frequently to assess the momentum of your gift.

Allow me to share a few things that will greatly help you sustain your gift:

Set high standards - During one of his Unleash the Power Within (UPW) sessions, Tony Robbins indicated that when he was interviewing Michael Jordaan and asked him what it was that made him the greatest. Michael said that he demanded more from himself than any other person could demand from him. This, I believe should be the type of attitude you need to have in order to maintain higher levels of performance in your talent or gift. Whenever you set a standard and achieve it, set another higher standard to achieve and in that way, you will become unstoppable with your gift. Keep working hard on yourself even when no one is watching and remember that people are rewarded in public for what they practice in private.

- **Discipline** - It will continually be important that you maintain a good focus for the sake of your gift. Yes and no are going to be two of the most important answers you will need to give to sustain your gift. Whatever answer you give will surely determine your destiny. Which is why to refine your gift you are going to have to learn to say no and yes with precision. You will learn to say no without the feeling of guilt in order to protect your gift. You will need to distinguish the difference between the good things and the right things. Not all things that are good are right for your gift. When you come across such things, then you must be willing to let even the good opportunities pass because they are not right for your gift.

- **Persevere** - Your gift will always come across some opposition, failures and disappointment as indicated in the previous section. These, however, should not discourage you but should rather propel you to even greater heights. Embrace these like the eagle, which strives during periods of very heavy storms. Although easier said than done, you must not take any of the disappointments and failures personally. Look at them as what they are, mere events, and events come and go but you remain. If you encounter failure, it is okay. Just take a few steps back to make the necessary corrections where possible, after all nobody is perfect. Remember you win some and you lose some, and that is just the nature of life.
- **Work Hard** - You need to really work hard on your gift. You must realise that the mere fact that you have a gift does not exonerate you from working hard at your gift. You need to make sure you refine your gift. In fact, you need to work harder than any person you know in your field of gift or talent. Tim Notke once said this about talent, "hard work beats talent if talent doesn't work hard". You must also make sure you keep abreast with any latest developments in your specific field.

Advice on choices for careers - Whenever you decide on a career path or qualification to study towards, I would suggest that you please make sure that this is preceded by your purpose. In other words, your career should be dictated by your purpose and gifts.

Remember, your job may give you an income, but your gift has the potential to give you a fortune. My sincere suggestion to you would be that you use your current job as a stepping-stone towards your gift or purpose. This may require that you put in some extra hours after work to develop your gift on a regular basis. "We have been damaged greatly by our culture, we have been damaged greatly by our society, and we have been damaged greatly by our education system because they have actually been conditioning us that we are only here to find a job, pay our bills and die." - Dr Myles Munroe

As I conclude, I encourage you to please go back and dream again, and be childlike once more. You must no longer live a life ruled by limitations. Be yourself and set yourself free from the chains of bondage. You are not a mistake but are destined for a greater purpose in life. Try not to look for employment but rather seek deployment for your purpose. Do not wait for big breaks, start where you are and never despise small beginnings.

Once you discover your purpose and your gift, you are now ready to create a preferable image of your future self, only when you.

Chapter Three
Find Your Vision and Follow it

"Some men see things as they are and say why? I dream of things that never were and ask why not?"

- George Bernard Shaw

Now that you have identified your purpose and ways to develop and maintain your gift, we can divulge into how to construct the vision needed in order to reach or accomplish the purpose. A vision is the product of a purpose, it stems from it, and it is your purpose in picture or images. Furthermore, it is the ability to see things not as they are but as they could be. It is to see further than your eyes can see. It is the ability to envision your purpose in your mind by faith and begin to imagine it. Your vision is the promise of what you shall one day be. It is an inspiring picture of your purpose, which energises your mind, will and emotions. All working together towards empowering you to do everything you can to achieve it. A dream worth pursuing is a picture and blueprint of a person's potential. It is a seed of possibility planted in the soul of a human being, which calls him or her to pursue a unique path to the realization of his or her purpose.

Every great person in history had a vision, be it Nelson Mandela, Andrew Carnegie, Steve Jobs, Mahatma Gandhi, Isaac Newton, Mother Teresa, Martin Luther Jnr, Albert Einstein, Abraham Lincoln, and the Wright Brothers. They all could not see it, could not smell it, could not taste it nor feel it but the vision was alive in their own minds. It was so alive in their minds that they began to live as if that future reality was happening in their present moment. A vision gives clarity to a purpose, it fuels it. A good question to ask regarding having a vision is can you see your vision with such clarity? Whether you have answered yes or no, my hope for you is that things may become easy for you to identify what your vision could be.

As we have already established, a vision is when you can see, not with your eyes but with your heart, an image of your future better self as your purpose manifests itself. Sight is a function of the eyes while vision is a function of the mind. He who cherishes a beautiful vision in his heart will one day realise it.

Your vision must distinguish you from other people who are in the similar field. Hence, there is no need to envy or compete with others when it comes to your vision because your vision is your unique quest to manifest. Remember that your vision, just like your fingerprint is meant to distinguish you from every other person in the world.

It is important to also realise the need for focus when it comes to your vision. *"Whether you are young, middle aged or older, if you don't have a clear vision, you are going to be distracted by every other business in the world because the world is an extremely busy place,"* - Myles Munroe. Do not undermine the power of clarity. Having a clear and guiding vision will assist you to stay on track even when tempted by other less important things.

If you were to build a new home for your family, you know that you would be interested in the blueprint or house plan for your new home and you would make sure that the builders conform to the blueprint. Driven by excitement after seeing the blueprint, you would then ensure that you get the best material for your new house. Now the question is, if a plan or blueprint is so important in a cause such as building a house, would you then honestly leave this important task to guess work?

If you have driven or walked past a construction site, you may recall seeing a picture of a completed building just next to the construction site. This picture or image is there to provide passerby's with insight of what is yet to come. I can safely say that this image could also serve as a great motivation for the builders of the new development. I doubt that there is a company that will willingly agree to any construction without having seen the envisioned idea in a form of a completed plan or blueprint.

Your vision sets you free from the limitation of what the eyes can see and makes you leap into the liberty of what the heart can feel through your subconscious mind. It makes the current suffering and disappointments bearable because you have seen a preferable future and have held on to that idea. Furthermore, it generates hope during despair and endurance during tribulations. "For the joy set before him he endured the cross, scorning its shame, and sat down at the right hand of the throne of God," Hebrew 12:2. This is the reason people with a vision are always optimistic because they have seen something far better than where they are.

A clear vision is what inspired the Wright brothers to be the world's first aviation pioneers. Can you for a moment try to imagine what people could have said to them at that time when they heard of their idea? I can just imagine the number of criticisms they received and the comments on how crazy that idea seemed to be but despite all that, the two brothers persisted.

Thanks to them, our lives are made much easier with the use of airplanes.

A clear vision of freedom and democracy is what propelled Nelson Mandela to endure 27 years in prison fighting against a vicious system but ultimately won the battle. People with visions become very stubborn and will not allow anything to deter them from reaching their preferred destinations.

It is said that where there is no vision, the people perish, and as much as this may not refer to people literally dying but a person without a vision is stuck or will be limited to the current condition of their lives. While on the other hand people with visions, whom are often, called visionaries, their imaginary world is more real than the concrete reality around them.

Document your vision - Your vision must be written down. A vision not written down is just a mere wish and often leads to disappointments. Whenever you write the vision statement, you need to write it in first person. This enables you to charge yourself into taking control of your destiny by constructing realistic plans that reflect the characteristics and concepts you have identified. Refer back to the journaling in the previous chapter, on tips on how to complete this process.

"Write the vision and make it plain on tablets, that he may run who reads it. For the vision is yet for an appointed time, but at the end it will speak and will not lie. Though it tarries, wait for it. Because it will surely come it will not tarry," Habakkuk 2:2

The moment you write out a statement of your purpose, you would have planted an image of the vision firmly into your subconscious mind. Through some process that even the most enlightened scientists have not yet discovered. Nature causes your subconscious mind to use that future image or vision as a blueprint that guides the major portion of your thoughts, ideas and efforts towards the attainment of your objective. This is a strange abstract truth. Something that cannot be weighted or even meditated upon – but it is the truth, nevertheless.

Here are a few facts about developing your vision:

- **Phasal** – Your vision will be manifested through a series of phases and the timeline of these phases may be monthly, quarterly or yearly. Nonetheless, it is important to ensure that you celebrate all these small wins (through goal achievements) and enjoy the process. This is a journey to relish. Do not wait until you have that big business but opt to celebrate even the little things like registering the business, getting approvals for sponsorship and so forth.
- **Revision** – You must adjust your vision on an ongoing basis. Certain things might come along during your journey, and you may need to adjust those few things. Your vision must be very flexible.
- **Evaluation** – You must be able to evaluate your progress to assess if you are still on the right track or not. If you went off track, you need to retrace your steps and realign with your future self.
- **Vision board** – This is a powerful tool to use to manifest your life desires. It is one of the most important tools in utilising the law of attraction. It is more than merely cutting words and images from magazines hoping to attract you desires. This tool turns your dreams into reality. It constantly reminds you of your life goals. It is a very integral part of the process of visualisation, which is nearly as powerful as performing the act itself. A vision or dream board is simply a

tool used to help clarify, concentrate and maintain focus on a specific life goal. It displays, shows, or represents anything you want to become or do. It helps us in remembering our life purpose in the ever-busy lives that we live. By creating a vision board and placing it in a visible spot where you can see it daily, you create the opportunity for consistent visualisation to train your mind, body and spirit into manifesting your desires.

The 6 P's (Principles) to fulfilling your vision:

1. **Patience** - As it is profoundly said, patience is a virtue. Patience brings with it peace and calm amid uncertainty. People with patience are most likely to win in their endeavors while it ensures the ultimate success in their vision. You must always remember that your duty is to find and develop your vision. Forces beyond your control shall provide the ways and means for its fulfilment. As much as you need timelines on your goals (covered below), these dates should always be rearranged, as and when required.
2. **Passion** – Passionate people are the people who have discovered something more important than life itself. Without passion, you will not be successful in any undertaking. You must be willing to go after your vision no matter what it takes. Although it saddens you to be where you are, however, knowing that you want to be where your true joy and inspiration is fuels your passion. Your vision then overcomes any resistance.
3. **Prioritisation** – "Everything is permissible for me - But not all things are beneficial," - 1 Corinthians 6:12. Your priorities will help you make better decisions; it will allow you to say no to certain lesser opportunities even if there are benefits in them. You should not accept all opportunities that come

along, even if they are good for you. As explained previously, you must distinguish between the good and right things..

4. **People's influence and association** - You will need people around you who believe in dreams that are even bigger than your own so that you can keep stirring up your vision. To live and pursue your vision, you will need to understand that proximity is power and really be mindful of whomever you surround yourself with. Your vision is not meant to be fulfilled by you alone. There will be people you will need to work with to make your vision a reality. You will always need positive people in your life for your vision to manifest. Your vision will stir up like-minded visionaries to work with you. Your association will truly determine your visions fulfilment. It is often said that you become like those with whom you spend your time. Peoples influence can be described in two ways, subtle and powerful. For example, you may spend time with people and they may have a subtle effect on you but their impact will be very powerful in your life. This is where we sometimes refer to peer pressure, which is simply other people's influence over a person's life. This occurs at all levels of growth, young or old. Which is why it is important to choose friends who are walking in the same direction as you. Do not allow people to come into your life only to change your vision. "Learn from others but don't become them," - Myles Munroe. The ultimate joy of life is to be yourself.

5. **Perseverance** – Having a vision has a way of waking up opposition. Your vision will always be tested for its authenticity. Moreover, life will throw many challenges at you to test your resolve. You will need to take those challenges as stepping-stones to greater heights. Knowing this, it then makes you embrace the challenges as they come. The minute you want to follow your vision you may be surprised at how suddenly there is so much opposition working against it.

Without a vision, nobody will bother you. The minute this happens you need not worry because it is expected that some people will start gossiping and saying bad things about you. Once that happens, know that you are now moving from their level of comfort zone, which is why such is expected. Criticism may come from friends, the public or even your family. Reality is it is sad that at times the most criticism may come from your close family members. Regardless, opposition at most times is a sign that you are doing something important with your life. If you study the history of most people who changed the world, you will realise that most of them had to declare independence from other people's expectations. Opposition is proof of the universal law of relativity that states that the universe will test your intention for its authenticity. Instead of noting them as problems, these tests should rather be seen as opportunities. There are certain people you might have grown up with who may no longer be relevant in your life as you pursue your vision. You can outgrow your friends and that is acceptable. Why? Well simply because you are no longer speaking the same language anymore. Once you have unlocked your purpose, discovered your why and have insight on the destination you want to be at. It then becomes even more important to start establishing steps towards that destination to ensure you achieve your purpose. You are now ready to.

Chapter Four
Set Meaningful Goals

"Focus on your goals, not your fears. Focus like a laser beam on your goals." - Roy T. Bennett

A soccer game is planned between two teams and the game is set for the weekend. Everyone is anticipating a very good game including the supporters from both teams. The day of the game arrives and fans flock into the stadium and meanwhile in the dressing rooms, the coaches go through the game plan once more with their team players. Before you know it, it is now time for the game. Eager to be on the field, the players and the coaches leave their dressing rooms to be met by cheering sounds and vuvuzelas from their supporters who are filled with great expectations. However, when the teams enter the pitch, they see something sinister on the field. There are no goal posts! Shocked by what their eyes are seeing, the players and coaching staff become frustrated and annoyed by the absence of the goal posts. Surely, this was very upsetting because they know that there is no way the match can go on without the goal posts.

Now, if we were to apply the above example to how human beings function, it is very shocking to realise that many people live their lives without goal posts. They are aware that they need to play the game called life but they have no goals to aim at. A goal is the object of a person's ambition or effort, an aim or desired result. It is a plan or something you expect to do. It is thus, imperative that whoever you are, wherever you are and whatever you do, you ought to have set goals. Having goals allows you to have direction in life and you are giving meaning to your vision. With definite goals, you release your power and sooner than you realise, things will start happening in your life.

It is said that a person without a goal is like a ship without a rudder. In addition to that, I recall the profound words of Arnold Schwarzenegger, "without goals you are like a ship that leaves the harbor and end nowhere". While it is very important to discover your purpose and have a vision for this purpose, it is even critical to set up action steps that will propel you towards the vision because a purpose and a vision without goals is as good as daydreaming. As we know, daydreaming most likely leads to disappointments.

Goals can be set for different aspects of your life, for example, physical, spiritual, financial, career, relationship, personal and mental goals. This is to ensure that your goals cover the entire spectrum of your life and that you live a balanced life.

When you set goals, something inside you will start saying, "let's go do it". It is important that your goals be big goals because it takes a big goal to create the excitement necessary for maximizing accomplishment. There is no excitement in mediocrity or in keeping up with everyone. You must set BIG, clear and meaningful goals while aiming to achieve each one of them. You must see it big before you can make it big. A wise man once said, "Make no small plan for they have no capacity to stir men's soul."

Rules for Goal Setting - The following are rules or criteria you should follow to ensure that you develop meaningful goals:

- **Present Tense** - Your goals should be stated in the present tense and not in future tense. Though tempting to state them in future tense because they have not yet materialised, please make sure it is in the present tense, because it is important to think as though it is already happening. This is a very important element as it relates to how your mind works. Examples are; if you want to be successful do not say, "I want to be successful" which is in future tense but rather say, "I am successful". In other words, you must say it as if it is already happening or you have already achieved the goal.
- **Specific** - Goals that are vague or non-specific are a recipe for failure. To decide that you are going to lose twenty pounds or get out of debt, for instance, it is a nice idea, but provides you with no guidance on how you can achieve that. Think about how much easier it would be to accomplish the weight loss plan if you knew exactly what you were going to do in order to lose the weight. You will start accomplishing more than you thought possible. If you are running a business and wish to increase your sales by 20% this year, for instance, you will need to come up with a plan.
- **Positive Terms** - Your goals should be stated in positive terms to ensure that you have proper focus. Positive terms simply means that you do not say things like "I do not want to be broke", because in as much as this may sound like what you want but what it says is what you do not want. Instead, you should rather use positive terms such as "I have more money". This has clear focus on what you want rather than what you do not want.
- **Be in Control** - Whenever you set up a goal it must be something that will allow you to have full control over the outcome. You do not have to rely on circumstances or other people to achieve your goal.

- **Time Based** - A goal must have the time for its intended achievement. You may have a monthly, yearly, or a 5-10 year goal plan.
- **Congruency** - You need to picture yourself having had achieved your goal to see if it would make you feel the way you intended to feel when you developed the goal.

There is a certain goal setting technique, which I personally use to set and review my own goals of which I will share with you below. I would recommend that you choose to focus on the following areas in order to develop your goals: **personal development, career/business/economic, adventure/toys and contribution goals.**

For each of these goals write as much as you possibly can. Keep your pen or pencil ready. Do not worry about how it will come to pass, just keep writing.

- Personal Development:

Step 1. - Write all the personal development goals you wish to achieve, social, spiritual or mental etc. You can write as many as you want. Write everything and anything you can imagine, do not restrict yourself.

Step 2. - Now, next to each goal write the number for the timeline of its achievement.

Step 3. - Now, choose one and the most important goal in this category.

Take a few minutes to write about why you are so committed to achieving this specific goal by asking yourself the following questions; Why is the goal important to me? What will I gain by achieving it?

What will I miss out on if I do not achieve it? Is the reason strong enough to follow through?

- Career/Business/Economical Goals:

Step 1. - Write all the career/business/economic goals you wish to achieve. This simply refers to the type of career or job you wish to have, the kind and magnitude of business you intend to establish or the amount of money you wish to make or the investment you wish to invest in. Write everything and anything you can imagine, do not restrict yourself.

Step 2. - Now, next to each goal write the number for the timeline of its achievement.

Step 3. - Now, choose one and the most important goal in this category.

Once done, take a few minutes to write about why you are so committed to achieving this goal. Why is this goal important to me? What will I gain by achieving it? What will I miss out on if I didn't achieve it? What are the strong enough reasons to make sure I follow through with my goal?

- Adventure/Toy Goals:

Step 1. - Write all the adventure/toy goals you wish to build, create or buy (house or car)? Events or seminars you wish to attend or the exotic places you want to visit? Write everything and anything you can imagine and do not restrict yourself.

Step 2. - Now, next to each goal write the number for the timeline of its achievement.

Step 3. - Now, choose one and the most important goal in this category.

Take a few minutes to write about why you are so committed to achieving this goal. Why is this goal important to me? What will I gain by achieving it? What will I miss out on if I didn't achieve it? What are the strong enough reasons to make sure that I follow through with my goal?

- Contribution Goals:

Step 1. - Write all the contribution goals you wish to contribute towards humanity, what you wish to give back or create, etc.

Step 2. - Now, next to each goal write the number for the timeline of its achievement.

Step 3. - Now, choose one and the most important goal in this category.

Now take a few minutes to write about why you are so committed to achieving this goal. Why is this goal important to me? What will I gain by achieving it? What will I miss out on if I did not achieve it? What are the strong enough reasons to make sure that I follow through with my goal?

After you are done with listing and prioritising your goals. List all the resources you currently have that will aid you towards achieving your dreams. What character traits will you need to have to achieve these goals - skills, resources, behaviour, training, beliefs, etc.?

For each goal, write down what you would have to do first to accomplish this dream. State what may prevent you from having the things you desire right now and what you can do to change it.

Sustaining the momentum - Create momentum, take immediate action - once done start doing something today. Even if it is a phone call or web check but whatever it is, do something towards achieving each one of your goals.

Check on these goals daily and each time you look at them, imagine yourself having had achieved them and not forgetting the feeling that comes with the achievement. You should also make sure that you review these goals at least once in every six months to check their validity as well as to see if there are things you might need to add or change. Remember that your goals should allow for flexibility. The other thing you will want to do is to make sure that you celebrate any achievement that brings you closer to your goals, even the smallest wins. This will encourage you to want to make the other goals happen. Anyway, why would you want to achieve a goal when there is no reward for it?

Now that we know about our reason for existence and the importance of setting goals. Let us get into understanding our own personal powers through the mind, power and consciousness.

Chapter Five

The Secret Knowledge of Power

"If there is no enemy within the enemy outside can do us no harm." - African Proverb

A group of international Life Coaches and Psychologists were working with the German car manufacture to conduct a driving experiment with two drivers, Mike and Henry. They are provided with two similar sport cars for this experiment. The purpose of the experiment is to examine the mental strength of each driver under the same environment conditions. The race will be between two towns with a 70 km distance between them. The driver assessor assures both drivers that the road conditions are near perfect, no traffic is anticipated and the weather condition is good. Furthermore, the drivers were assured that there would not be any traffic officials on the road and therefore, no regulated speed limit.

Prior to the race, one of the drivers is strictly denied the consumption of any negative news but is only exposed to motivational and inspirational content while the other driver is granted the permission to engage in ANY content.

Both drivers have vast experience as race car drivers. However, when the race began the team started to notice that both cars are moving at a similar speed. Conversely, after a few minutes something changed as now Mike's car was moving ahead of Henry's car. The gap between them began to increase as the two drivers moved closer to the end of the race. At the end of it all, Mike had obviously won the race. While the team interviewed the two men, they noticed some difference in their mental conditions. Mike always fantasized and enjoyed the adrenalin that came with driving a sport car. He believed that was the best moment of his life and claimed it felt like heaven. On the contrary, Henry gave a different view and belief about his experience in the race. Reason being, he had in previous weeks, exposed himself to news in and around the country. He had heard and seen a few accidents associated with sport cars and this resulted in him having the fear for driving at high speed, hence his poor performance during the race. The results then clearly showed that people could have the same external and environmental conditions but still produce different results. In addition, performance is also not based on the external things, but it is based on the inner game, what a person thinks and believes.

The Inner World - This is the inner reality of your thoughts, emotions or feelings, including beliefs and attitudes. In the world of the mind, thought is the only action. Although thought is the only action of the mind, it is also the most important action in every living person.

We relate to the inner world through the subconscious mind. It is through this mind that we are all connected to the universal mind or infinite intelligence that is brought into relation with the infinite constructive forces of the universe.

The world within is the practical world in which men and women of power generate courage, hope, enthusiasm, confidence, trust and faith by which they are given the fine intelligence to see the vision and the practical skill to make the vision real. What comes to us in the outer world is what we already possess in the inner world. Harmony in the world means the ability to control our thoughts and to determine for ourselves how any experience is to affect us.

The Outer World - "The world without is a reflection of the world within," - Charles F. Haanel. The outer world reflects what already exists in the inner world. The outer world is the reality of people, places, circumstances, things and events. It is the avenue for the unfoldment of whatever already exists in your world within. Unfortunately, for most people, as stated above, there is an absolute dominance of the outer world of appearance on the inner world, and the inner world is merely used to react to what happens in the outer world, hence, people never realise their true power.

We relate to the outer world through the objective mind, also referred to as the conscious mind. The brain is the organ of the mind, and the cerebro-spinal system of nerves puts us in conscious communication with every part of the body. The system of nerves responds to every sensation of the five senses, which is light, heat, odour, sound and taste.

The inner world controls the outer world. The complete understanding of the two worlds is perfect knowledge. The key is to understand the inner world and use it to rule the outer world. The inner world is the cause while the outer world is the effect. The outer world reflects the inner world. The outer conditions mirror the inner consciousness. Which is why the inner world, and the outer world are not two separate worlds, but they are connected. They are two different levels of the same world. As within, so without.

"Any idea that is held in the mind, that is emphasised, that is either feared or revered, will begin at once to cloth itself in the most convenient and appropriate form available." - Andrew Carnegie

If you look around you, wherever you live and whatever circle of society you are part of, you will notice that most people live in the outer world or the world without. Those who are more enlightened, however, are intensely involved with the inner world or the world within. They realise - as you will too - that the inner world creates the outer world. This is something that less than 10% of the world's population are aware of.

Have you ever wondered what it is that makes one person very great and yet another mediocre? I mean two people can face the same circumstance or condition as illustrated above, but their response could be so different that you will end up thinking that they did not experience the same thing. Well, the answer lies in the type of consciousness that everyone has on his or her life.

Whatever you are experiencing right now is an unfoldment of whatever lies in your inner world. In fact, it is impossible for anything to manifest in your life if it does not exist in your world within.

Now let me share my own story of the use of the inner world. Growing up as a boy, I disliked going to school a lot. The situation got so bad that together with my older brother from my uncle's side, (his father and my father are brothers from the same mother), we used to hide at a nearby hill not far off from the primary school we were in at the time.

To be precise, I was in standard one (Grade 3) when I skipped school and obviously, I failed the grade and had to repeat it. Fortunately, for me this was at a stage when my family decided to relocate from that village to another village called Itireleng. I was awarded the opportunity to rewrite my life and repeat the grade at a new village. My attitude towards school took a turn for the better and it was evident as I began to confidently pass all my subjects including receiving remarkable marks for all grades. Allow me to say that the change was mainly due to changing my belief system that I started having at the time. Just something to take note of, throughout these times in my family, my mother used to brew some liquor just to make ends meet for us. It was during these times that I started to ask myself questions regarding my school performance and wondered if there was any way at all that I could change. In doing so, I would be one of the best pupils like those I saw and were leading in my class.

Initially I used to think that the best pupils in class were simply the gifted few and born to be that way but then things started to change when I challenged myself to see the possibilities to become one of those best pupils myself. To any other person who knew me at that time, this would have been likened to daydreaming or impossibility because at that time I was just the average, academically struggling pupil in class.

To cut a long story short, once my belief became a conviction, I then started to see myself sitting at that number one spot in class. It was then that I started seeing all possibilities for making this a reality. With my new belief, my study habits changed completely. It was not long before I too was part of the top five in class. Without a doubt that certainly made my confidence grow immensely and I was able to top my own grades, that by the time I was in form 4 (Grade 11), I was ultimately the top student in matric at my school. An internal change in my belief changed everything concerning my studies.

At the time, I was obviously not aware of the power of the mind and the power of the inner world. In hindsight, I realise that all the conditions that existed when I struggled at school remained the same but what changed was the changes in my inner world of beliefs. If I could do this, I realise that anyone can do it too.

It therefore, makes it easy to conclude that success and failures are predictable, they are subject to this secret knowledge of life and one of the greatest secrets is.

Chapter Six
The Power of Your Subconscious Mind

"Whatever you plant in your subconscious mind and nourish with repetition and emotion will one day become your reality."

- Earl Nightingale

Now that you have insight into the powers you possess through the inner world and the knowledge of how this world is controlled by the subconscious mind. We will discuss in more detail how this inner world works, how we can fully acknowledge and apply it in our lives in order to experience life in its fullest.

One of the most critical things about your mind is that through proper knowledge, you can make the mind work in your favor but again, with neglect the very same mind can work terribly against you. You may be a bit surprised that many people use only 5% of their brains and that is on a daily basis. Which brings me to the question of what happens to the rest of the 95%? Well, the answer lies in the understanding of what this chapter is about. It is the understanding of the mind that distinguishes ordinary people from great people.

To understand these powers let me start by saying that all of us have brains and when the brain is in action it is referred to as the mind. The mind has two distinctive characteristics. All men and women who effectively use their minds know the difference between these two functions. One of the characteristics is the objective function that is for reasoning, to rationalise or provide logic. This mind is called the conscious mind while the other part is the subjective function that is for our habits and programs, is known as the subconscious mind. The conscious mind is the waking mind and is active when we are awake, and the subconscious mind is the sleeping mind and works all the time. It works 24/7 and is the mind that never rests.

The subconscious mind is responsible for the functioning of all our bodily functions, like the heart, our blood circulation, breathing, hair growth, walking etc. It controls 95% of our lives. Actions by the subconscious mind happen without your influence.

The relationship between the two minds is that the subconscious mind accepts any thoughts presented to it by the conscious mind if you believe the thought as true. It is reported that we filter around 2 million bits of information per second down to smaller chunks of information. This means that the data available to your central nervous system will go through a process of deletion, distortion and generalisation for you to make sense of all the information. Thus, the unimportant data is filtered out by a bundle of nerves at the core of the brain stem, the control centre, which is called the Reticular Activating System or RAS for short. The Reticular Activating System is the main reason why goal setting works. By writing down your goals and focusing on them, you then communicate to your RAS what information you deem important and valuable. There is an incredible amount of processing going on behind the scenes. Still, the RAS is excellent at recognising and using the information to achieve your goals better than you could on a conscious level. Your RAS will start to connect the dots and immediately work to find ways to align yourself with your goals and dreams. It will manifest any idea presented through conviction (strong belief/faith), expectancy and repetition. It does not argue or reason like the conscious mind. Instead, it will act as instructed by the conscious mind. Once your subconscious mind accepts the statement or whatever it is you believe as a fact it will proceed to do everything possible to bring it to pass. Your thoughts can be compared to the seed, good or bad, when sown in the subconscious mind it will bear fruits of its own kind in your life. It forms new programs from thoughts with strong feelings or emotions for example love, joy, fear, anger, sadness, gratitude, excitement, etc. It does all this through our habits. It has been said that our lives are a printout of our own stored programs in the mind. It is, therefore, important that you train your conscious mind to think thoughts of success, happiness, health, and prosperity and to weed out or get rid of the feelings of fear, anger, doubt and worry.

Here are some few facts around the functions of the subconscious mind:

Habit Mind - A habit is a redundant set of automatic, unconscious thoughts, behaviours and emotions that are acquired through repetition. A habit is when your body knows how to do something without involving the brain. It is when you do something without thinking twice about it. This is when your mind has formed comfort zones, which are often hard to change. It has been said that 95% of the things we do by the time we become adults are memorised sets of behaviours, attitude and perceptions that are hard wired into our brains like a computer program. This is the reason some people can say they want to be rich or wealthy but find themselves still poor or broke. The reason is that these people are engaging 5% of their mind with their wish while the subconscious program is on the lack set up. Our habits make or break us as individuals. They run our lives.

Habits vs intellectuality (academic knowledge) - I have always wondered why there are so many people who are academically educated but struggle to make ends meet financially. I can testify to being one of these people at one stage in my life. Most people have acquired the highest level of academic qualifications and are regarded as the smartest people with good reasoning capacity but behold, most of them struggle financially and finally, through this knowledge I came to understand why this is so. You see, the reason this happens is that education deals with knowledge and awareness to the conscious mind, which controls 5% of our mind function, and less powerful than the subconscious mind. These people have financial lack programs installed within over a lifetime and no amount of education can change that. Unless they engage their inner self and change, the programs through practicing mind renewal techniques. On the other hand, there may be people who never went far with their education and who are often deemed as not clever. However, these people live within abundance. Most of them could fortunately have grown within environments where wealth programs were instilled in their inner mind and that now serves as their insurance to abundance.

Comfort zone - Your subconscious mind, through some specialised neurons, form comfort zones and causes you to feel emotionally and physically uncomfortable whenever you attempt to do anything new or different or even attempt to change any of your established patterns of behavior. The sense of fear and discomfort are psychological signs that your subconscious has been activated. The tendency to commit to these patterns is one reason why habits can be so hard to break. However, when you learn to purposefully create such patterns, you can harness the power of habit and purposefully instill new comfort zones to which your subconscious will adapt to.

You can feel your subconscious pulling you back toward your comfort zone each time you try something new, even if that thing is good for you. Even thinking about doing something different from what you are accustomed to will make you feel tense and uneasy.

Superior men and women are always stretching themselves and pushing themselves out of their comfort zones. They are very aware how quickly the comfort zone, in any area, becomes a rut. They know that complacency is the great enemy of creativity and future possibilities.

Value of hard work - To get out of your comfort zone, you must be willing to feel awkward and uncomfortable in doing new things the first few times around. Remember that if anything is worth doing, it is worth doing poorly until you get a feel for it, until you develop a new comfort zone at a new, higher level of competence. Anything that you struggle to do, even though it is good, it is a clear sign that you do not have the program that supports it and that is when you need to put some work into making sure that you instill this in your subconscious mind for it to create the new program. Keep in mind that an installation of any new program will be through repetition. The more you work hard at it, the mind will start forming new neurological connections to make sure that the thought, action or behavior starts to form new comfort zones. It is, therefore, crucial that you realise that working on your mind does not excuse you from working hard.

Access to Infinite Intelligence - The subconscious mind is the only mind that has access to the infinite intelligence (the mind of the supernatural or creative force or the mind of the Creator). There is in fact sufficient evidence to support the belief that the subconscious mind is the connecting link between the finite mind of man and infinite intelligence. You can bring into your life more power, wealth, health, happiness and more joy by learning to contact and release the hidden power of your subconscious mind.

The infinite intelligence of the subconscious mind can reveal to you everything you need to know at every moment of time and point of space through intuition for as long as you are open-minded and receptive.

No Sense of Humor - Our subconscious mind has no sense of humor; it plays no jokes and cannot tell the difference between reality and an imagined thought or image. This means you should not make a joke out of the bad things happening in your life because the mind might interpret that as what you aim to experience.

Tape Recorder and Memory Bank - The subconscious mind is a data bank for everything that has happened in your entire life. It can remember anything that happened in your life.

It stores your beliefs, your previous experience, your memories, your skills and so forth. Everything that you have seen, done or thought of is also there.

Cannot Recognise No or Not - An epidemic worse than any plaque that humankind has ever seen and has been raging on for centuries is the "don't want" epidemic. Most of the people have grown accustomed to saying things they do not want. Words like "I don't want problems" are very common in our society. Instead of uttering those words, it would be better to say what you want instead like "I want peace". Unfortunately, the subconscious mind cannot recognise the words "no" or "not". The reason for this is that the subconscious mind stores information as images and if you say, "I don't want to fail" the image that appears in your mind is of failures hence you will continue to fail.

Present Tense - The subconscious mind only knows the now, the present is the only tense that matters. You must say things or see them in the present tense because it cannot tell the difference between imagination and reality. An example of this is, if you want to be rich then you must say, "I am rich" instead of "I want to be rich". The second statement spoke into the future while the first points addressed the present. Hence, we say you attract the things you think about most of the time. Repetition creates new beliefs in your subconscious mind. You will remember that I indicated earlier that all your goals should be stated in the present tense, thus the reason why you ought to do so.

The Farmer Gardener and the Fertile land Garden - To understand how the two minds function you need to think of yourself as the farmer gardener who has a fertile land on which anything can be planted. Remember, I said anything! The gardener in this case will be the conscious mind while the fertile soil is the subconscious mind. Now remember that anything the gardener plants will grow in the garden, be it a good seed or bad seed, flowers or thorns. Anything will grow if these are planted in the garden. The soil will ensure that there is growth and will not discriminate but will let any seed grow.

Real and Imaginary Acts - The subconscious mind does not know the difference between what is real and what is imagined. This means that you could trick your subconscious mind into believing whatever good you want to experience in your life. You can influence your subconscious mind by simply acting as if or behaving as if you already have what you desire to have or that whatever you desire is already a reality. The problem here is that most people unfortunately create images of things they do not like or the things they fear and hence, they are most likely to experience lack.

The Wild Monkey - The best comparison of the subconscious mind is to a wild monkey. It can run rampage the whole day, as it does not tire easily. Moreover, it can bring random pieces of information to the main part of the brain, most of which will be negative. You could consciously make it get busy with achieving your goals and bringing you the information that you need in order to succeed (opportunities). The only thing you must do is to give this wild monkey a purpose or something to work on.

No Idle Mind - The subconscious mind cannot remain idle. If you fail to plant desires and dreams in your subconscious mind, it will feed upon the thoughts that reach it because of your neglect.

Voluntary Injection - It is important to note that negative emotions like, fear, jealousy and hatred voluntarily inject themselves into our thoughts and into the subconscious mind. This is the reason why so many people are poor because the requirement for poverty is simply not engaging the subconscious mind with positive, powerful and harmonious thoughts. On the contrary, the positive emotions must be injected through proper techniques in order to influence the subconscious mind to act. It is your duty to guard against negative thoughts and use affirmations to stop these negative thoughts.

Programming or Conditioning of the Mind - This is how our subconscious mind was and continues to be conditioned. Which is why it is of high importance to be aware of these influential mechanisms and to apply those that can work in your favour:

Auto or Self Suggestions - This practice involves sending thoughts to your subconscious mind with suggestions on what it should manifest. This can be done consciously or unconsciously by yourself or by other people. There are two types of suggestions to the mind and the first one is called self or autosuggestion. It comprises of self-administered stimuli, which reach one's mind through the five senses: touch, taste, sight, smell and hearing. The dominating thoughts that remain in the conscious mind (negative or positive), make their way to the subconscious mind and influence it. A thought dominates if a strong emotion (faith, fear, love and so on) empowers it.

The second suggestion, which is what you hear or get from other sources including people, media etc. it is called hetero suggestion.

Examples of hetero suggestions are newspapers and news that could sow seeds of fear, anxiety and uncertainty. If accepted these thoughts of fear could cause you to lose the will to live. Good news is that you can reject these destructive suggestions. This is when it is important to have daily affirmations, which you can refer to at any time.

It is important to note that most of the hetero suggestions happened in our childhood or teen years with the sole purpose to control you or instill fear. For some people these suggestions unfortunately, continue to occur in their adult lives.

It is important to take note that suggestions can be either positive or negative. Positive suggestions will lead to positive outcomes while negative suggestions will lead to negative outcomes. While there are people that use positive suggestions, please note that unfortunately, most people use negative suggestions against themselves unconsciously.

One of the known examples of negative hetero suggestions are the suggestions we most received since childhood in the form of words like "it's getting worse", "life is just difficult", "you are too old", "things are difficult nowadays" etc. Suggestions such as these can devastate your life unless you decide to use constructive autosuggestions to reprogram your mind.

It is important to remember that hetero suggestions have no power over you except the power you give it through your acceptance and belief in them. You must give mental consent to the thought and accept it for it to become your thought. This means you have the capacity to choose. Choose a good life.

Feedback from the Subconscious Mind - As we have already established, the communication between the conscious and the subconscious mind is a two-way communication. You give your subconscious mind tasks, desires and goals. In addition, it gives back information, opportunities and ideas.

Intuition - Intuition, put simply, is the knowledge of something without thinking of it beforehand. It is the guiding "inner voice", which always knows the truth - what is ultimately best for you, in all situations. Intuition shows up in many ways, sometimes in dreams, flashes of mental imagery, positive and negative vibes, coincidence, synchronicity, insight, and gut feelings.

Richard Branson trusts it. Steve Jobs said it was more powerful than intellect. Warren Buffet uses it and Albert Einstein once called it the only real valuable thing. Moreover, Forbes once said, "Intuition is the highest form of intelligence".

Intuition is the ability to understand something instinctively, without the need for conscious reasoning. Similar words are hunch, instinct, sixth sense or gut feeling. Intuition is the key to everything in life; hence, you must trust your instincts.

Intuition exists in all of us, whether we acknowledge it or not. The more we can learn about it the more we can use it to shape our lives for the better. It is very quick, instinctual and effortless. The intuition is set in operation if you concentrate on some matter of importance. It arrives at the conclusion without assistance from the objective mind. It solves problems that are beyond the grasp of the reasoning mind or power.

The intuition must be recognised and appreciated; if it is given a good welcome when it stops by it will come again like a relentless visitor. The more cordial the welcome, the more frequent the visit. However, if ignored it will shy away and will seldomly be at hand to help. Intuition sometimes comes to people at awkward times like during a shower, upon waking up, taking a walk or during performing any other light duty. Which brings sense to what Albert Einstein once said, "Why do I always get my ideas during a shower?"

Next, let us continue to delve into the powers of the inner world through.

Chapter Seven

Change Your Thoughts, Change Your Life

"As you think, so shall you be." - Wayne Dyer

There has never been nothing so liberating to me like the knowledge that I become what I think about most of the time. Most philosophers over the years have had some disagreements on certain aspects of their profession but this is one point they all agreed upon. Proverbs 23:7 says, "As a man thinketh in his heart, so is he". In consideration of that, most of us have grown under the wrong belief that what we have become is a result of other people's doing and therefore, we have no control on what has happened to us up to date.

Most people will blame their circumstances or hold their parents responsible for how life has turned out for them. Nothing could be further from the truth than that. We have brought ourselves to where we are now. We are fully responsible for all the circumstances and conditions in our lives.

Our thoughts can be likened to the action of planting seeds in the ground or garden and the result being that we always get the fruits of whatever seed we have planted. This means that we cannot simply think negative thoughts and then expect to experience positive outcomes. That will be against the law of reaping and sowing. Thoughts are the function of the mind while feelings are the function of the heart or body. Therefore, to live a fulfilling life, we need to master the two. Your life now is a pure reflection of your past thoughts. It is a signal of the dominating thoughts you have had all these previous years.

Thoughts and Circumstances - Every thought seed that is sown or allowed to grow in the mind and to take root, will produce its own kind. Blossoming eventually, into acts bearing its own fruits of opportunities and circumstances. In his book, 'As a Man Thinketh' James Allen said, "Good thoughts bear good fruits, bad thoughts bear bad fruits". Furthermore, he also indicated that circumstances do not make the man but that they reveal him to himself. Your wishes and prayers are answered when they harmonise with your thoughts and actions. To fight against circumstances is just a waste of your energy because you are fighting effect without engaging the cause, which is lying within. If your thought is constructive and harmonious then the results will be good. However, if your thoughts are destructive or inharmonious the results will be bad.

You Reap What You Sow - Good thoughts cannot produce bad results and bad thoughts cannot produce good results because that will be against the universal laws of nature, just as a banana seed cannot produce an apple as a fruit. The circumstances, which a man encounters with suffering, are mostly the results of disharmony within the mind. One of the greatest discoveries for man is that the universe is always right and as you change your thoughts towards things and other people, the very same people will change towards you. In as much as when you change the way you look at things, the things you look at change. Your thoughts can not be kept secret because they soon turn into your habits and these habits crystalises into your circumstances. Meaning that people may not know what you are thinking but through your circumstances, it will be easy to guess your thought process.

Thoughts and Achievement - *"All that a person achieves and all that he fails to achieve is the direct result of his own thoughts. A person's purity, weakness and impurity are his own and not another person's, they are brought about by him or herself and not by another,"* James Allen.

The more he continues to think so he shall continue to be. It is everyone's responsibility to uplift themselves through good thoughts, even a strong person cannot lift a weaker person without their will; they must first become strong for themselves. Only a person can change their own condition and not by another person. It remains the responsibility of every human being to lift their thought before they can achieve anything, even if it is in the material world. It is by lifting his thoughts that man can achieve greater success, attain more blessings and sustain such success.

Type of Emotions - Negative thoughts develop weak habits, which lead to failure and slavery dependence; and lazy thoughts develop habits of dishonesty, which lead to circumstances of poverty. Hateful thoughts develop habits of violence and accusation, which culminates into injury and persecution.

On the other hand, good thoughts develop habits of grace and kindness that lead to goodness; thoughts of courage, self-reliance and decision develop good habits, which lead to success, plenty and freedom. Energetic thoughts develop into habits of cleanliness, which lead to pleasantness; while gentle and forgiving thoughts develop placid habits that lead to preservative circumstances. Lastly, loving and unselfish thoughts develop habits of self-forgetfulness and harmony that leads to riches. Your assignment is to ensure that you make a conscious effort to monitor whatever goes into your mind and make sure these are good thoughts.

"Whatsoever things are true, whatsoever things are honest, whatsoever things are just, whatsoever things are lovely, and for good report, if anything is excellent and praiseworthy – think of such things" Philippians 4:8. Whenever the negative thought comes in simply cancel it with a positive thought or just exaggerate it as merely false.

Thoughts and Emotions - The relationship between thoughts and emotions is quite strong. Everything starts with a thought and then a corresponding feeling follows it. If you take out the brain, then you have no feelings at all. The body is an instrument of the mind. Emotions are energy in motion and the quality of your emotions determines the quality of your life. Successful people are those who are or have mastered their emotions. Once a thought is conceived, it will send chemical signage to the heart to create a corresponding feeling or emotion. A change of feelings is a change of destiny, and when you change your emotions, you change your life. Therefore, if you think something is difficult this will send a corresponding chemical signage to the body to create a feeling of unhappiness and despondency. Likewise, if you think of good things in your life, it will send feelings of excitement and happiness in your life. Which is why you cannot think greater than your emotions, the two must align. Your thoughts affect your body chemistry.

Thought Energy Vibration - One of the well-accepted realities is at a microscopic level where everything is in constant motion, vibrating at a specific frequency. This applies to matter but also on human or personal frequency as well. Nothing stays the same. Vibration simply means your emotional state. Our frequencies carry information just like in televisions, radios and cell phones, which all transmit information at certain frequencies. To get different type of information all you must do is change the frequency and the TV or radio will give you a different station (information). We are constantly radiating energy around us, and we attract whatever becomes our vibrational match from the universe. Contrary to previous beliefs, we do not get what we want but we only receive what we radiate. You receive or experience love by first radiating love to others. Thus, the same applies with receiving or experiencing peace by first radiating the peace to others and the opposite is true. You will experience negative thoughts and emotions if you radiate those negative thoughts and emotions. Which is why I ponder about the thought that if it is true that we only experience that which we radiate, then what can one do to have an influx of money? The answer to that is that you must first give away money in order to make space to receive more. I used to be a critic to the tithing principle that states giving 10% of your "income". However, through the understanding of this knowledge my perception changed for the better. I now give 10% of any income I get. You may gift your 10% to a charity, feeding scheme or spiritual center/church of your choice. The key is to give. It is one of the secrets to accumulating wealth. An act done by those who already have obtained wealth. Once you do this all the universal forces will work in your favor.

This is one of the main reasons to why some people would have a lot of money but cannot hold onto it that before they realise, it is gone. You may have heard stories of people who won the lottery but after a few months, they are back to where they were. The unfortunate reason for this is that although they might have attained the money, they were most likely operating at the very low frequency levels of lack opposite to that of wealth and money. Wealth and abundance operate at a very high frequency level of constant joy, love, appreciation and gratitude.

Living in The Past - Remember in the previous chapter, one of the characters of the subconscious mind is that it operates like a memory bank where all the events of the past, including from our childhood, are stored. Now the danger of that is that people can tap into these old banks to remember old thoughts and events, and these are then associated with emotions of which are by-products of past experiences. This means that most people because of the nature of their thoughts and feelings are living in the past. A person will remember a painful or disappointing event that occurred in the past. As they continue to ponder about this event in their minds, their bodies will generate a similar emotion to the body and because the body is the unconscious mind and cannot tell the difference between what is real or not. It then thinks that this is what the person wants to experience and as a result, you begin to live in the past. Meaning your mind and body are thinking and feeling everything as if the events of that past are of present. Remember that your thoughts and feelings create the state you are in, meaning that if you think life is bad, you start to feel sad and worried and anyone who sees you at that time will notice that you are sad. It is often said that 90% of the thoughts you think today, are made up of the things you thought of yesterday. It is no wonder why most people live their lives without seeing any improvements to their experiences. One of the reasons why people find it difficult to detach from that is because our minds operate through habits. People can develop the habit of thinking negative old memories, which will activate similar negative emotions and the circle will continue.

Emotions: Survival and creative emotions - According to neuroscientists there are two types of feelings or emotions. The first being survival or stress emotions. These types of feelings include anger, fear, frustration, anxiety, hatred, guilt, embarrassment, unworthiness, blame, doubt and competition. The reason these are called stress hormones is that these are emotions that cause most people to have constant stress levels in their lives. The two stress hormones are adrenaline, which increases heart rate and you blood pressure and boosts energy supplies and also cortisol, the primary stress hormone which increases glucose (sugar) in the bloodstream. Furthermore, 70% of the people live on stress hormones every day and now you wonder why the world is where it is now. The reason so many people live under stress hormones is that they are functioning on their survival state of mind, which aims at protecting us against future harm, hence it will always go back to these emotions to make sure that we are ready to act should the event reoccur. This is called an emergency or survival mode. People are always anticipating the worst-case scenario and they want to make sure they are prepared should another bad occur. There are far too many people living in fear, or anxiety of what will happen next and are constantly blaming other people for their misfortunes. These survival emotions carry with them very low energy and low frequencies which makes it difficult to manifest anything productive in life. Whenever you are carrying these emotions, they are bound to attract other energies at the same level of vibrational frequency match from the universe; these include misery, pain, lack, limitation and so forth.

Addiction of Stress Hormones - One of the problems with these survival emotions is that people become addicted to them to a level that a person with hatred will always want to find something that will feed their need for hatred. If they hated a colleague and the colleague happens to no longer work at the same company, they will always find someone else to hate. That is the power of survival emotions. A person addicted to anger will always find something to be angry about to feed their addiction.

Extended Stress Hormones - Naturally, all creatures can withstand a shorter period of stress hormones and in fact, it is normal for anyone to be well prepared for any emergency to react accordingly through flight, freeze or fight modes. The problem occurs when someone switches these hormones for an extended period than supposed to. That is when you know that the person is headed for a disaster because no living creature can withstand being in an emergency mode for longer periods. When hyenas chase a springbok and it happens to escape, the springbok will go back to normal grazing and thereby move from the survival mode. The same is true for people; no person can live in fear or worry all the time and not experience negative reactions from the universe.

Long-term Memories - Whenever we experience an emotion for a certain period, it is called the refractory period. If the emotion is carried for several days, then the person is said to be having a certain attitude or is in a certain mood. If this experience carries on for months, then the person is said to be having a temperament. When you ask them why they are always angry they will tell you that something happened to them months back that they have not been able to let it go of. If this emotional experience carries on for years, then the person is said to have a personality trait or characteristics of an angry person. From there onwards, they are known as an angry person. The good news is that all these emotional experiences can be changed through mindset techniques discussed in the next chapters.

Our challenge and assignment then is to manage and make sure we have very shortened refractory periods. What this is saying is that you may sympathise with people with very sad emotions but always make sure their emotions do not absorb you. It is also fine to express our negative emotions at times like being sad. We are human after all, and we go through disappointments and sorrow, but the trick is to ensure that we shorten the refractory period. Advise where need be but do not make a mistake of occupying their state of being because that will not serve you instead it will only work towards bringing your energy down.

Effects of Thoughts and Emotions on Your Health and Body - As mentioned before, the body is the instrument of the mind. It acts based on the mental activities from the brain. The body obeys the operation of the mind, whether they be deliberately chosen or automatically expressed. Most diseases and health issues, just like circumstances, are rooted in how you think. Thoughts of sickness reveal themselves into a sick body. While thoughts of fear have long been known to kill men as fast as a bullet can. Those who live in fear of a disease are the same people who will soon get it. Clean thoughts create clean habits.

According to author Dr. Joe Dispensa, it has been scientifically proven that stress hormones regulate genes and causes diseases in a long run. Knowing this it becomes crucial that we manage and limit these emotions as much as we possibly can. On the positive side, it then becomes obvious that the opposite emotions will cause us to be well. What is also scary is that human beings, due to the size of our brains (neocortex), are capable of self-inflicting stress by thought alone. On the contrary to this, it is also possible for you to improve or upregulate your genes and be well through your thoughts alone. For as long as men have negative and unclean thoughts, he will continue to generate impure and septic blood. To perfect your body, stand guard at the gate of your mind.

Let us take a detailed look at a few of the emotions, which Wayne Dyer calls erogenous zones, for us to understand them better and know how they affect our lives. The aim here is for us to learn how to eliminate these emotions.

Guilty and Worry Emotions - The two emotions are on either extreme side of the line. One is an emotion for the things we are worry could negatively happen in our lives in the future and the other (guilt), is when we have survival emotions from things that happened to us in the past. One is in reference to past events while the other is focused on future events and mostly, the worst-case scenarios. With guilt, many people suffer from imposed guilt enforced by other people like family and friends. This type of guilt happens due to people saying or doing things that make us feel guilty. Things like "You failed at school and have wasted your parent's money!", or "You should be ashamed of yourself for doing this and that". All these sentiments are meant to make you feel some sort of guilt. Other types of guilt sentiments are those we have about our own past. People carry guilt from whatever wrong things they did in the past. Others will have guilt from having spent money on things that are not tangible and becoming broke because of misusing money. The guilt of not doing enough for the family or your parents may lead one to carry some guilt with them for a long time. All these guilt feelings serve nothing but only trap and immobilise you from moving ahead in life.

The other emotion of worry happens when people become worried about things possibly going wrong in the future. This is conjuring of the worst-case scenarios for the future, and it is not to be confused with planning (vision and goals), for the future, which are good things to do. Being a worrier is when you are anticipating and being anxious for bad things in the future. This act unfortunately, does not change anything in that future but instead, it only makes you not enjoy living in the present moment.

All that the above as well as the other survival emotions do, is to siphon your energy to the past (guilt) and future (worry), and then you are left with little to no energy to deal with the present moment. Remember that where focus goes, energy flows and so your energy depletes and is wasted in the process. Leaving you feeling exhausted, depressed and overwhelmed.

Blame - Blame is another one of the survival emotions you can use as a devise whenever you do not want to take responsibility for something in your life. It is a complete waste of time and no matter how much fault you may find with another person and regardless of how much you blame them, it will not change you. The only thing that blame will do is take the focus away from you when you want to explain your frustration and unhappiness. Blame may make you succeed in not thinking about the issue, but you will not succeed in changing whatever it is you are putting blame on someone else for.

Anger - This is also another one of the survival emotions, which you do not have to possess. It serves no purpose nor does it have anything to do with you being happy. Anger comes in forms of hostility, rage or even striking someone or through deafening silence. Anger, just like the other survival emotions is immobilizing and caused by someone wishing that the world and the people in it were different, and to some extent they wish others to be more like themselves. Anger is a habit and hence, some people have the addiction for being angry. These people will be angry at anything in their lives and if you take the source of that anger away, they are bound to find something or someone else to be angry at. Anger is a result of thinking, it is not something that simply happens to you, it is a choice, and as long as you think of anger as part of what it means to be a human being, you have a reason to accept it and avoid working on it.

Whenever you are choosing anger as a response to someone else's behavior, you are withholding from that person their right to be what they choose. In your head, you may be asking yourself, "Why can't he/she be more like me?" Every time you choose anger when you run into someone or something you don't like you are deciding to be hurt or be immobilised because of reality. Now being upset about things that are not going to change is actually not necessary and instead of being angry, you can choose to think of others as having a right to be different from what you prefer.

Instead of using anger as an immobilizing agent, I suggest that you rather use it as a catalyst to make changes in your life. You can use anger to change the current quality of your life because most people in history made serious changes with the anger they felt towards their conditions at that particular time. Most of the people who fought for liberation in this country were buoyed up by the anger of the apartheid system, which fueled their need to see change happen for the better. There are people I know who have resigned from companies after being angered by the working conditions they considered unfair. In fact, you can use anger to propel you towards your purpose buy detecting things that make you angry or sad when done wrong.

The other types of emotions are called creative emotions and they include love, joy, excitement, bliss and gratitude. These emotions carry with them very high energy and vibrate at a high frequency, and because frequencies carry information, they transmit very positive information back to us from the universe. People with these emotions are very powerful and influential and these are the type of people that are said to have an aura around them. Whenever you are around them, you can actually feel their energy. All things seem to be possible when you are around them. The challenge is to make sure you avoid the survival emotions and only operate and use creative emotions to make your life better and more productive.

How to change - The hardest part about change is that, once programmed, our bodies are so hard wired that whenever a person tries to change and do something new then the body gets surprised and asks, "We have been doing this for all these years and now you just want to change like that. Maybe put it away for another day?" The same thought will lead you to the same behavior patterns that will lead to the same experience and result in the same emotions. The body in this case has become the leader over the mind; the student has now become the master.

Change will only be realised through the installation of a new neurological software top that replaces the hardware. To do this you have to be in the unknown territory. This is when people find themselves in an unfamiliar and unknown territory, firing and wiring new neurons. The best time to create a new future is through the unknown and not the known. Think about how the seed grows. It has to be planted in unknown ground (soil), to be nourished and induce growth. You can put the seed on a surface or table and have all the possible hopes for it, but it will not grow in this foreign environment.

Some of the most effective ways to changing negative thinking is through focus, the power of language and physiology. It is so amazing that one can quickly change the way you feel by simply changing your focus. It is important to focus on things you have other than the things you do not have. Whenever you feel a bit of negativity, just try to think of all the things you have done in your life and are proud of. The mere thinking of these things will greatly improve your emotional state, just try it and see how you feel thereafter. The other way is to focus on the things which you are grateful for because remember it is impossible to feel grateful and be angry, or to worry and be sad at the same time.

Concerning the use of your physiology, this refers to you using your own body to change the way you feel. Next time you see a depressed or sad person try to see how their body looks. Their head is mostly likely going to be dropped, chest in and their breathing very shallow. To change how you feel all you need to do is to simply change the direction of the above-mentioned body parts. Have your head up straight, chest out and take a few deep breaths, then exhale. Regarding the language, make sure you use positive language most of the time. Instead of saying, it is difficult rather say it is challenging, instead of saying things like I am stressed out, rather say I need to challenge my creativity. Some of the other ways include meditation and having a sense of humor and finding ways to include humor and laughter in your life, watching comedy. Avoid unhealthy ways of managing your stress such as alcohol, tobacco, drugs or excess food

If there is one negative emotion that has had devastating effects which I have witnessed in the lives of the people I know and encountered throughout my lifetime, and I am encouraging you to really.

Chapter Eight
Let Go of Your Fears
"Cowards die many times before their deaths; the valiant never taste of death but once." - William Shakespeare

I know that I have touched on the subject of fear in certain sections in the previous chapters. However, the subject at hand is one that requires its own discussion simply because this is one of the biggest, if not the only major obstacle that people face when they are supposed to be making life changing decisions.

Fear can paralyse or immobilise a person to a point that their dreams and potential remain in tatters. Fear kills dreams. It kills hope and it leaves people in hospital beds, plus it makes you age faster. Fear can make you accommodate mediocrity as a way of life. It is no wonder that the words "fear not" appears 365 times in the bible and that alone will make you see why this is such a very important topic to discuss separately. Fear is one of the highest negative feelings or emotions related to the high stress levels of human beings. Winston Churchill had this to say about it, "there is nothing to fear but fear itself". It is fear that has made cemeteries extremely rich with gifts and talents that were never realised. I know of so many people who go to their jobs simply because they have to pay their bills and are afraid of changing or even trying to pursue their dreams. These people have made peace with lack as an acceptable norm and the mere thought of significant change paralyses them. The amount of uncertainty on change becomes unbearable for them. "Fear is the most subtle and destructive of all human diseases," said

Smiley Blanton, renowned author and colleague of Norman Vincent Peale.

When it comes to fear it does not matter, how talented or dissatisfied you are with your current life. Most people continue to stroll along at the workplace they hate because they are afraid of making a change. Many people are afraid of rejection, disappointments, uncertainty and failures. However, the reality is that there is no person who is not afraid. We all get scared at times in our lives, but the difference is what you do when you feel afraid; after all, that is what distinguishes great men from ordinary men.

Personal development author Zig Ziglar said, "Fear is false evidence appearing real". It is an illusion that we create in our minds, and he further argues that fear is just a bias that we carry around with us and cannot move past it. Fear keeps us from trying out new things and settling for the comfort zone with the belief that everything is safe there, but the unfortunate thing is that there is no growth there.

Different Responses to Fear:

When faced with a fearful situation, people can choose to respond in three ways. Through one of the three F's hardwired into our subconscious mind and it is our natural response that keeps us alive. This is the same as what the animals have as well. When faced with a fearful situation most animals would respond in either flight, freeze or fight mode.

Freeze - Having grown up in the village, there were times when we would be herding cattle or hunting for some springbok when suddenly we would come across certain animals. When these animals would see you, they would freeze and pretend to be dead as a way of defending themselves. A porcupine for example, would hide within itself to protect itself against the intruder. Now freezing is evident in most people as well who are doing certain jobs or are in relationships they do not like. Instead of changing the narrative, they will just go along with the groove hoping things will somehow change in their favour. They fade away as they blend into the background. They would ignore any signs that show them that there are no more opportunities within that particular spectrum but still put their heads in the sand. In most situations, the situation remains stagnant. Freezing means no progress.

As a former employee myself, I have witnessed so many people staying in jobs and positions they don't like but with the inner hope that things will one day change but most of the time these people eventually reach retirement and all that is left is regret for what could have been. It is shocking to know how many people go to their jobs and most of the time whenever anything is happening, they feel unhappy about what comes to their minds which is the possibility of being fired. People are forever making sure that they perform just enough to remain safe for any possible loss of their jobs due to being fired or retrenchment. The question that remains now is if you spend most of the time worried about the possibility of losing your job when do you really have time to be creative within that job?

Flight - Most animals would run away from a predator; a buffalo would run like crazy whenever it sees a lion attacking and after a while, it would relax once it notices that the lion is out of site. Most people prefer to run away from opportunities, challenges or situations that demand more effort and hard work from them. Unfortunately, running away is not going to solve your problems if you want to achieve the life of your dreams. Flight mode, just like the freeze mode will not solve your problems.

Fight - Of all the responses, this one gets even the onlooker entertained. When an animal feels it must either protect itself as a way of protecting its family or little ones, it then decides to stand its ground. The animal digs in deep and fights with all it has. Whether it wins or loses, they will still give it a fight. Now this is the attitude you must have in order to succeed in living your dreams. You just have to have the instinct to fight for what you want and what you deserve. There is no running away or freezing up. The good thing about giving it a fight is that even if you lose you would have learned valuable lessons in the process and you will definitely know how to do it better next time.

Courage and Grit - Courage in its simplest meaning refers to the ability to keep going even in the presence of fear. People with courage can boldly face fear and give everything they have. To some people such people might deemed as fearless, but nothing could be further from the truth. Courageous people are also afraid at times but the difference with them is that they do not let fear stop them, meaning despite being afraid, they continue to do it anyway. They never back down from a fight, and always appear cool, calm and composed amid adversity. Courageous people know and are afraid that they may be risking their financial position, their future, livelihoods, or reputation, etc. but this does not stop them. Fear does not deter them. Therefore, I urge you to have courage, look at your fears and face them regardless! No matter what happens you will come out stronger than when you went into the fight. People with grit on the other side will push through even when it feels uncomfortable to do so. They give everything they have until the last round. They may face dispassion of assets or bankruptcy but still push through it all just to see their dreams come true. A combination of the two make a person enormously powerful.

Cultivate Faith - If there was any best way to deal with the fear of uncertainty of the future, this would have to be through faith. You are going to have top belief in the things not yet seen by the naked eye and see them as your new reality. It is often said that fear and faith are poor bedfellows, where one exists the other one does not, meaning that you cannot be afraid and have faith at the same time. It is either you are afraid, or you have faith. To truly experience change and alter your life for the better you are going to have to have the evidence of things not yet seen.

Chapter Nine

Create Your Reality Through Imagination

"Imagination is everything, it is a preview to life's coming attraction."
- Albert Einstein

Imagination is explained as the act or power of forming a mental image of something not present to the senses or never before wholly perceived in reality. It is one of the powerful ways of supercharging our subconscious mind into action and it would actually be nearly impossible to find your vision without applying the art of imagination. Therefore, imagination is the ability of the mind to be creative or resourceful. Most of us have been brought up to think and believe that what we see, hear and touch with our senses is the ultimate truth but the reality is that all that we mostly see in this world are facts of whatever that was once imagined by someone at some point in life.

Imagination is the very gateway to reality itself. I am yet to see anything in the world that was not once imagined by someone. For all that exist was once imagined. If you believe in this reality, would it then not be a good idea to know how to use it? If everything that was ever formed was created through imagination, then it would be correct to say that through imagination, we have the power to be anything we desire to be. This now becomes evident that man can actually create the type of life he or she desires and to the contrary, this is occurs irrespective of the facts (from our senses and reasoning).

Once you know or are aware of this truth, you start to realise that only as we live by imagination, can we truly be said to have lived at all because living within the world of facts, reason and our senses puts us at the mercy of the world. Furthermore, we become victims of our own circumstances. I must mention here that there is nothing extraordinary about this imagination process because all of us do imagine things from time to time. The difference here is that most people use imagination unconsciously while others put imagination to use by imagining the worst-case scenarios. The idea here is to use imagination consciously for your own benefit.

To do that we, therefore, need to use our imagination by acting as if or assuming that our wishes are already granted or fulfilled. We refer to this way of imagination as thinking from the end. If you would sustain this feeling of your wish fulfilled, you could make your assumption to harden into facts. Neville Goddard, one of the greatest teachers on imagination once said, "Experience has convinced me that an assumption, though false, if persisted in will harden into fact, that continuous imagination is sufficient for all things and all my reasonable plans and actions will never make up for my lack of continuous imagination".

It is important to realise here that the person with a conscious imagination does not deny the reality of the world of senses. What he or she knows is that it is the inner world of continuous imagination that is the force by which the world of senses is brought to pass. It is therefore, truly marvelous and a blessing to discover that you can imagine yourself into the state of your fulfilled desire and escape from the bondage of facts around us in the external world.

It is of even greater importance to know and acknowledge that imagination in itself may not bear any fruit, unless there is an accompanying belief in whatever you are imagining. For example, if I imagine myself to be successful but on the other side, I feel and believe that it is difficult to obtain success then I will be sabotaging the same wish I sought to achieve and may end up not achieve it at all. Consequently, it becomes important that you match your imagination with your beliefs. These beliefs are sometimes called states, which is what we believe and consent to be true. Also, realise that nothing can be realised unless the mind accepts it. The matching or fusion of our imagination with our states is the ultimate shaping of our world. Since our body and imagination form our states and the imagination process of the mind, which therefore, means that there must be cooperation between our mind and heart. You must imagine yourself in the state of your fulfilled desire.

Determined or persistent imagination, thinking from the end, is the beginning of all miracles. You must be able to make the future, the present in your imagination in order to wisely and consciously create favorable circumstances. Thinking from the state desired is the only known creative living and the ignorance of this will only lead to bondage and the becoming of victims to circumstances. "Let the weak say "I am strong", in other words, let the weak assume "I am strong" and so shall it be.

Nothing can stop a person who can think from the end. Most of the greatest leaders of our time knew this, either consciously or unconsciously. For them it did not matter what they went through or what their current conditions were. All that mattered was what they saw in their imagination. They knew that the world is a manifestation of the mental activities that goes on within themselves and so they controlled the end from which they thought. With their focus on the end, they lived with the confidence that they will experience this end in flesh as well.

To ensure that success is achieved, three conditions must be satisfied, and these are:

1. A longing and intense desire to achieve a specific objective. You must know what you want to achieve in your life and hence, the importance of the beginning of this book to focus on the purpose, vision and goals.
2. Secondly, to get the best out of your imagination you must cultivate physical immobility meaning that you must learn the art of being still. Most, if not all of the suggestions happen during stillness or quietness.
3. The third and final condition to ensure success is to have the feeling ahead of the experience.

At the ultimate end, it should be so refreshing to know and realise that the life we live is a controllable thing and that we have control over our destiny. The practice of imagination is achieved through repetitively practicing the following.

Chapter Ten
Auto-hypnosis

"In a dream, in a vision of the night, when deep sleep falls upon men, while slumbering on their beds, then He opens the ears of men, and seals their instruction." - Job 33:15-16

With proper repetition, this is perhaps the most effective way to reprogram the subconscious mind. Unfortunately, most of us were conditioned with certain disempowering beliefs during the early stages in our lives. While these negative programs may not have been intentional, however, their unfortunate consequences live with individuals for years after that and some for their entire lifetime.

It is said that 95% of our lives stem from the programs of how we live life and what we acquire in the first 7 years of our lives and that is the reason why some people are well off or rich while others struggle to survive. Every infant and child within the ages of 0-7 years goes through the hypnosis phase, which is a tender age where the child's brain is in a lower vibrational frequency. Their brains only use the subconscious mind, and they have no conscious knowledge of anything and so they record all the things being said and done by those around them. One can liken this behaviour to an empty tape cassette with no recording on it. Their brain at that stage operates under the theta brain wave state (discussed in the next chapter under visualization). Theta is also known as hypnosis and this is the highest level where the subconscious mind is receptive to new suggestions, just like a new cassette.

Now can you imagine a child who grows under very negative conditions where they are constantly told, "life is difficult", "money does not grow on trees", "the world is a bad place", and soforth. The problem becomes evident when the child is all grown up and attempts to climb up the ladder of success. They may be shocked at how illusive success is in their lives and this happens simply because of the program that were recorded at their hypnosis phase. A phase that taught them to see things as difficult to attain because as explained in the previous chapter, thoughts become things. If you can recall, 95% of our lives is the subconscious mind.

This is the reason you may find an intellect with so much knowledge and reasoning being poor or not financially well off. It is the same reason why many people are merely surviving financially. They are operating more on the 5% of their brain and the programs keep running as per recorded tapes. In order to assess the type of programs instilled in your mind; all you have to do is check the things that you have to do with difficulty. This serves as a sign that your instilled programs do not support it and it is the intention of this book to reprogram those programs for you to the one you want and will prove to be beneficial.

The good news, if not the greatest news ever is that even though our minds were programmed at an early age through hypnosis, thankfully we are provided with the same capabilities during our adult life stage just like that of young children. All of us go through what is called autohypnosis, which is the same stage that infants and children go through. It is called auto because you now have the ability to inject into your subconscious mind with whatever that you wish to experience.

This autohypnosis stage happens every time we are about to fall asleep or are in a sleepy drowsy state and our minds goes through the same theta state as seen in infants. It is advisable that before you fall asleep, you either put on earphones and listen to programs or podcasts, or read any book containing whatever you wish to experience in your life. This is one of the magnificent ways that indicate that there is a second chance in life.

A second chance granted to you to help you change your life to being the way you want it to be. We have the ability to correct the damage that was inflicted on us during our early years. This is a clear sign that indeed God is love and He loves us.

Chapter Eleven
Visualisation and Meditation

"What you visualise, you actualise and materialise."

- Jack Canfield

We often hear the words meditation and visualisation used interchangeably, but they are not entirely the same. Visualisation is the imaginative practice that activates and supercharges the subconscious mind and it involves the use of vivid images so that the scene is as real as possible. It is one of the most powerful techniques. You can use the technique to recondition or reprogramme your mind to cultivate whatever you wish to achieve in life. Meditation on the other hand is mostly the function of the soul or spirit. According to the Oxford English dictionary, mediation is the practice of thinking deeply in silence, especially for religious reasons or in attempt to calm your mind. Below is a breakdown of the differences and similarities between the two, and how each practice can be used to make your life better.

Differences - Meditation is a process that is more restful while visualisation is very active. There is a saying in meditation that says, "Doing more with less and letting go". This simply refers to the fact that this is the process where you just let go and let things be whereas the visualisation process requires you to concentrate on a particular goal or outcome to be achieved. Secondly, meditation calms the subconscious mind while visualisation reprograms it. Lastly, meditation moves you beyond consciousness into the state of being and is different from the waking, sleeping or dreaming states. By contrast, visualisation is more of a waking state practice. We are more fully conscious when it is happening. We guide our thoughts to visualise the best-case scenario or use our imagination to have a full-five sensory experience of how your next high-demand situation would ideally play out. Just as Olympic athletes use the visualisation method prior to competing in the games to improve their outcomes. I highly recommend that you incorporate the visualisation method as well prior to your big life events; be it public speaking, business negotiations, first dates or anytime you want to relax and perform at the top of your game.

Similarities - There are many similarities between these two techniques and hence, why some people use them interchangeably. However, both processes require you to be free from distractions and are most effective when used at a certain brain wave level. The processes requires that your eyes remain close throughout and both involve the controlling of your breath.

Visualisation - This is the chief technique of seeing and feeling yourself in your mind already being, doing and having the good that you desire. It is the creative dreaming of things into existence. It works like magic and will move you over many challenges in reaching for your goals. There is a saying that if you cannot see yourself wealthy, you will perish in your poverty or lack and if you cannot see yourself healthy, you will perish in your sickness. "If you cannot see it in your mind, you cannot see it in your hand," - Bob Procter. It is true that what you see (in your mind) is what you get (experience in your life).

The only way you are going to become what you want to be is by calling yourself that which you want to be. You do not have to concern yourself on how things will happen after visualization. This technique helps you bypass the how and calls those things that are not as though they were. The unseen become the seen. Your main concern should be knowing what you really want, i.e., your goals and dreams, and leave the how to your higher power through insights, intuitions and inspirations. Do not get caught up by the facts in your life because they will mislead you. Facts and conditions are not the truth of who you are.

Let us now look at the benefits you can attain from using this technique:

1. It activates your creative subconscious mind, which will start generating creative ideas to help achieve your goal.
2. It programs your brain to be more readily perceive and recognise the resources you will need to achieve your dreams.
3. It builds your internal motivation to take the necessary actions to achieve your dreams. You need to ask yourself the following questions: what would the feeling be like if I were the person I intend to be? What would I hear, what would I see?
4. It activates the law of attraction, thereby drawing into your life people, resources and circumstances you will need to achieve your goals.

To effectively apply the technique, the following is required:

- **Eliminate distractions** - This is the most important step that you need to apply for effective visualization. Make sure that you are sitting in a quiet space or room. Switch off your cell phone or put it on mute because you do not want to be tempted into answering calls during this process. I recommend that you choose a time perfect for you to meditate with hopefully fewer interruptions. It can be early in the morning or late in the evening.
- **Get comfortable** - After eliminating the distractions make sure that you are as comfortable as possible. You need to be able to feel relaxed and at ease. You may seat on a comfortable chair but avoid lying down as this might cause you to sleep during visualization.
- **Take deep, relaxed breaths** - Take a few deep breaths to enable you to relax. Make each breath longer and slower until you feel relaxed.
- **Keep it short, you do not need to visualise for hours** - This is important because some people might be discouraged to practice the visualization process because of the perception that you need to spend more time doing it. However, spending 5-10 minutes is sufficient. You will increase the time as you grow through meditating.
- **Keep it regular** - Visualising once a week is not going to do anything for your peace of mind. It needs to be frequent, especially in our overstuffed hustle and bustle world. You are much better off grabbing five minutes a day to center yourself instead of scheduling a half-hour

after your biweekly workout. We are bombarded with so much input on a daily basis and our emotions are constantly being overstimulated by injections of adrenaline and cortisol. Those precious five minutes every day is where the heavy lifting of emotional control is learned and allowed to perform its magic. If you can do more than five minutes on a daily basis, great! Do it. However, do not underestimate the benefit of daily practice.

- **Emotions and sens**es - Feel the emotions of the event ahead of the experience. Application of feeling fuels and supercharges the visualization process and makes sure that you involve all your five senses of smell, touch, sight, hearing and taste. Apply these to make the picture as real as possible. Always make sure you apply elevated emotions of joy, love and excitement during the process. You need to ask yourself the following questions. What would the feeling be like if I were the person I wish to be? If I had the things I wish to have, what would it be like? Imagine your wish fulfilled inspite of all the evidence of your senses and reason that denies it. All you need to do is to simply catch the mood.

Your brain is constantly using visualization in the process of simulating future experiences, but this process happens so naturally that you generally are not even aware of it. In the same way you usually are not aware that you are breathing. The problem is that if you are not aware of it then you are not actively directing the process. You can learn to use visualisation to actively create future simulations that can help you improve the goals that you set for yourself.

- **Importance of brain waves** - To follow this technique effectively it is important to understand how the brain works and hence it is important that I explain the different types of brain waves. These waves are periods occurring when the brain is either highly active, busy or very slow and receptive – this is the state of mind you want to be on when practicing visualisation. There are four types of brain waves.
- **The first one is the beta brain wave** - This is when the brain is very aroused and active. These are periods where our brains are very active which mostly happens when we are at work, doing projects or are at school and are required to have a lot of reasoning and logic. **The second** one is the alpha brain wave, and this is when the brain is slowing down from the high active period. These are times when our subconscious mind is receptive to suggestions. It is a time when most people slow down after work or school, preparing for supper and getting ready to sleep. **The third** brain wave is called the theta brain wave, and this happens immediately after the alpha state when we feel drowsy, sleepy and want to take a nap. This is the preferable state, and the best time to engage your subconscious mind. Many people who came up with an invention practised the art of engaging their minds at this state. It is when the conscious mind hands over to the subconscious mind; remember the subconscious mind works 24/7. Which is why it

becomes crucial to make sure that you lower your brain waves to the alpha state level before practising the visualisation process. This can be achieved through deep breathing (as per the steps detailed above) and focusing on all the good things in your life with gratitude.

- **Picture and Describe** - The more details you have in your visualisation the more real it will seem and the more it will increase performance as the brain starts to develop connections that result from the repeated visual image. Along with enhancing motivation, that increases the likelihood of taking an action toward your goal. The best way to create detail and enhance the quality of your simulation is to picture and describe it using all your senses. Keep adding in more detail until the process starts to feel as real as though you were experiencing it in the present moment.

- **Emotion Intensity** - Is a type of sensory-based representation in the brain. Because we know from the cognitive world that emotion is preceded by thought. When you feel something deeply, you have achieved a level of belief associated with it. You generally do not feel upset by something that you know is unreal or true. That is why we can watch upsetting fictional events on TV and a movie but not be overly traumatised or overwhelmed by the events. However, the more real or true you believe something to be, the more it has an emotional impact on you. To really enhance simulation, you want to create as much detail around it as you can so that you begin to feel the experience of it as if it were real. Once you have begun to feel it, you have crossed the threshold that leads to action and manifestation. One strategy that increases the emotional intensity of visual simulation is listening to music that matches the emotional intensity you are seeking as you are visualising your simulated future experience.

- **Exposure** - Since what you produce in your mind can only stem from what is stored there, it can be quite difficult to imagine something that has not already happened to you. It would be much more difficult to create a visual simulation of living in Mars than it would be to visualise yourself standing in your living room. Sometimes to create a more detailed and realistic visual simulation in your mind, you have to expose yourself to more detail in the outside world. For example, if you really dream of doing something you have never tried before like scuba diving, you may have a difficult time simulating a detailed experience because you do not have much to draw on. You will need to expose yourself to the experience of scuba diving. You may need to read books, watch videos, visit a scuba diving school, or talk to other people with scuba-diving experience. Anything that increases your knowledge and awareness of what the experience would be like can help you to have more data to draw upon when creating your own visual simulation.

- **Outcome** - You do not need to concern yourself with how things will turn out or the how part of the process. You simply need to trust the process. Supply follows demand meaning that as long as you know what you want and visualise it, it shall be provided for you. The means and ways of how the manifestation will happen will present itself to you for nature always creates the opportunities needed to fulfil the demands put upon it.

- **Timing** - The visualisation process can be done at any time of the day. You may choose the time that is convenient for you when you will be free and without disruptions. These may be early in the morning or in the evening but the condition is that it must be at the correct brain wave level, preferably the alpha state.
- **Faith** - If you can consciously follow and practice this technique, you will develop faith. The kind that knows the "substance of things hoped for, the evidence of things not seen". You will develop confidence, the kind that leads to courage and endurance; you will develop the power of concentration, which will make you exclude all thoughts except the ones that are associated with your purpose.
- **Repetition** - The clearness and accuracy will only be obtained through repetition. Repeat, repeat, repeat. That is the only and best secret to manifestation. Tony Robbins once said that repetition is the mother of skill and I guess that cannot be disputed.
- **Meditation** - While I have already touched on this subject in chapter 1, I will however, add a few interesting facts about mediation that are worthy of your attention. In chapter 1, most of the attention was on the intuitive nature of mediation to aid in knowing your life purpose and below are even more facts that are beneficial.

This is the best way to train your mind to be more precise, possess better quality, a higher functioning data filter and making you more of a mindful and happy person in the process.

When Albert Einstein was working on the modern theory of relativity, reports claimed that he would lay down on the couch waiting for inspirational thoughts to enter his mind. Many highly successful people are quoted giving much credit to meditation as their own secret "go-to" technique for generating transformative ideas. While we all want change in the world, the first thing that needs to change is ourselves. Meditation bridges that gap wonderfully by upgrading our minds and reprogramming our thoughts to easily manifest whatever end goal we desire - with abundance, health, and happiness being just at the center of the beginning.

Meditation is the world's very best deep mind training technique, allowing us quick, easy, and ready access to massive creativity, deep insight and super valuable information hidden underneath our conscious mind. Since meditation is in essence the process of digging down into the depths of your mind, session by session making your once inaccessible mind power to become suddenly available to your everyday consciousness.

Once activated our upgraded superman subconscious opens a whole new level of mind mastery, effectively and releasing much potential as a human being - while uprooting whatever limiting thoughts, beliefs and anything else that is keeping you from fulfilling your mission in life.

Meditation has a variety of benefits. Listed below are some of the benefits you may need to be aware of:

- **Longevity and life extension** - Most of the meditators look far younger than their actual age and they live much longer.
- **Weight loss** - Meditation can move anyone to his or her ideal body weight of looking fit and trim.
- **Success** - Most of the successful people credit their success to practicing mediation.
- **Intuition or gut feeling** – This was discussed in depth in the previous chapter on the subconscious mind. Intuition, put simply, is knowing something without thinking beforehand. It is the guiding "inner voice" that always knows the truth. What is ultimately best for you, in all situations. Intuition shows up in many forms, sometimes in dreams, flashes of mental imagery, positive & negative vibes, coincidence, synchronicity, insight and gut feelings, (refer back to chapter 1 above).
- **Anxiety** - It is such an anxiety reliever and in fact, it is often said that anxiety is no match to meditation.

Happiness and meditation are one.

- **Sleep and insomnia** - Meditation can conquer sleeping problems. It can help people with cases of insomnia sleep like a baby.
- **Creativity** - Mediation helps with inventions and creativity. Remember that many great people mentioned using it to induce intuition.
- **Depression** - Meditators are known to defeat depression with ease.

- **Problem solving and adaptability** - Mediation can help with problem solving and with adapting to the ever-changing world.

The diagram below details the relationship between different minds and the benefits of meditation in details:

Visualisation and Meditation

Anatomy Of The Mind: Meditation Gives You Access To Your Mind's Most Powerful Layers

Psychoanalytic Model

CONSCIOUS MIND
Beta Brainwaves

- We spend most time here
- Requires effort & energy
- Willpower
- Superficial ideas
- Educated mind
- Likes/Dislikes
- Intellectualism
- Stress source
- Insight
- Very small %
- Analytical
- Planning
- Beliefs
- Logic
- Says you aren't good enough
- Often in past or future tense
- Creator of limiting beliefs
- Mini-Processor
- Critical thought
- Very limited abilities
- Short term memory
- Self-esteem
- Judgemental
- Negative self-talk
- Thinking mind

SUBCONSCIOUS MIND
Alpha & Theta Brainwaves
Targeted By: *EquiSync* 1 & 2

- Programmed by your thoughts 24/7
- The true genius within, needs to be dug out
- Can melt away dysfunctional emotional issues
- All thoughts, feelings, experiences stored here
- Change your thoughts, change your life
- Accessed via meditation
- Knows the path to success
- Find your life passion
- Always "on"
- Higher self
- Incredibly smart
- Imaginative
- Visualization
- Intuition
- Lightning fast
- Life Solutions
- Mental imagery
- Deep Thought
- Untapped talents
- Stress-free
- Inner Peace
- Gut-feelings
- Super-Processor
- Self healing
- Incredibly powerful
- Limitless creativity
- Allows you to break mental barriers
- Tells you to relax, discover your deepest passion, make life what you truly desire
- Harnessing this power can dramatically change your life
- Temperamental
- Personality
- Sequential
- Rational
- Habits

UNCONSCIOUS MIND
Delta Brainwaves
Targeted By: *EquiSync* 3

- Highest self
- Spiritual connection
- Immune system
- Cellular memory
- Access to collective consciousness
- The 'core' of who you are
- Primal instinct
- Drives the dreaming state
- Incredible benefits
- Automatic function
- Body system regeneration
- Requires meditation to harness its power
- Permanent memory storage
- Wise
- Always in the "now"
- Unlimited space
- True desires
- Inventive

Deeper Meditation →

*** Results may vary from person to person

You can see from the diagram that meditation does provide us with many benefits and connects us with all our brain functions. As it is the only technique that affects all the functions of our mind.

When it comes to the details of steps for performing this technique, you will realise, as I said at the beginning, that these techniques have many similarities in comparison to visualisation and therefore, it comes as no surprise to refer to the visualisation process. Before practicing, please refer back to the first four steps under visualisation, which are the same practices used in meditation. I will only add steps that were not covered:

- Repeat steps 1-5 under visualization.
- Let your mind wander - Most people spend time worrying about the thoughts that come during meditation and some people might view this as failure but that is far from the truth. It is normal to have thoughts coming in during meditation and the secret is to never entertain or rather fight the thoughts.
- Allow calmness to blanket your mind - This may not be easy at the beginning because our mind is used to worrying about all the many things that are going on in our lives. Do not waste your precious meditating time by trying to solve problems during this exercise. Treat this moment as a sacred time spent with your Creator. Remember, you are trying to put your mind at ease here.

The steps above may seem like a lot, but it is all actually quite doable in just a few minutes each day. If you take those five or so minutes (especially parents), you will be amazed at the effect you will notice on your ability to get thin gs done. You will begin to find it easier to concentrate at work by shutting out distractions. You will also discover that you are much calmer and less excitable during the day, and that you will have better judgment when you go out at night. Since you are less stressed, you will find you have less need for excess drinking or to take recreational drugs. You will be more fun to be around and be better able to handle your partner, your kids or your social circle.

You will have more energy to commit to causes you believe in or to take up a hobby or a new activity you have wanted to try. Your co-workers might still be annoying, but you will be less angry about it and more capable of ignoring them. Furthermore, you will suffer less from depression and anxiety and experience less intense mood swings.

Meditation is not going to "cure" your problems. Instead, it gives you the ability to decide how to handle them by making you less vulnerable to overwhelming emotions. It gives you the ability to stop for a moment, take a breath, and look at a problem clearly and calmly. It will be the best five minutes you ever spent with yourself.

Powerful Combination - Finally, it is important to realise that the two techniques are not opponents but that anyone can use them with good results. In other words, you do not have to choose to either mediate or visualise because they can complement each other and at certain times, some people use them simultaneously.

Chapter Twelve
Supercharge Your Brain: Affirmations and Incantations

"Therefore, I tell you, whatever you ask for in prayer, believe that you already received it and it will be yours."- Mark 11:24

To affirm means that you are declaring something to be true. Affirmation is when you repeat a phrase to yourself, embedding it into your mind, until you believe it is true. It is a simple statement that you repeat to yourself either silently or aloud (whichever feels good to you) to reinforce your new belief system, goals and mind shift. It is one of the simplest techniques known to influence the subconscious mind and to ingrain new habits into your mind.

Affirmations can be done at any time and at any place. Use affirmations for whatever you want to manifest.

To affirm is to state it is so and as you maintain this attitude of mind as true, regardless of all evidence to the contrary, you will receive answers to whatever goal you are affirming. Repeating an affirmation, knowing what you are saying and why you are saying it, leads the mind to that state of consciousness where it accepts that which you state as true. Keep on affirming the truth of life until you get the subconscious reaction that satisfies.

At first, you do not need to believe what you are affirming. You only need to keep on repeating them until you start to believe it. Just like it has been said, if you keep telling yourself a lie you will start to believe it. Repetition breeds belief and new habits. As an example, just for a moment remember how you learnt about counting the alphabets from A to Z and the addition of numbers. All these were done through repetition instructed by teachers and over time, these became instilled into the subconscious mind until you were able to do it yourself. The same method applies with affirmations.

There are two kinds of affirmations; the first is the belief building affirmation. This is aimed at instilling and deepening a positive belief about yourself. It is like planting a seed of self-belief in the fertile soil of your subconscious mind and includes uttering words like "the universe is on my side". It involves things, events and life. The second one is called the desired result affirmation and this is stating specifically a desired goal as if you already achieved it. Its purpose is to activate the law of attraction and stimulate the subconscious mind to figure out how to achieve the goal. It is extremely powerful and becomes a powerful force when used in conjunction with visualization. Furthermore, it triggers the subconscious mind to come up with creative ideas for success.

Affirmations could be short and sweet and in that way, it will make it easy for you to repeat them at any time. One sentence is more preferable instead of a whole paragraph. Examples to use are I am successful or I have abundance, etc.

You must talk as if you have already attained that which you are affirming and use words such as "I have" and I am". An example of this is I am prosperous, I have abundance and I am wealthy, etc. The reason for this is because the subconscious mind only operates in the present tense, i.e., it does not recognise anything that is mentioned in past or future tense, like "I want to" or "I wanted this or that". Therefore, you must be incredibly careful when sending messages to the subconscious mind that everything is in the present tense.

When making affirmations always remember that, you are going to have to ignore your own conscious mind, which I can call the naysayers in this case. As a reasoning mind, it will always remind you that what you are saying is not true because it has not yet happened. Your work is to ignore this thinking and repeat your affirmation continuously, because deep down you know that the message you are sending must go to a mind that works on habits, that is the subconscious mind. Once it has accepted the repetitions it will manifest them because it works 95% of the time and has more power than your conscious mind.

Mantras - A mantra is explained as a sacred utterance, a word or group of words believed to have religious or spiritual powers. It is one of the extended versions of affirmations that are used with a rhythmic feel in them. Here you can have a long sentence or paragraph that rhymes with whatever you are affirming, for example, "I am so happy and grateful now that money comes to me in increasing quality, through multiple sources and on a continuous basis."

Personalised affirmations - Much as it is fine to use many of the available affirmations, it is even more critical that you create your own affirmation using your own special chosen words. You can do this by first getting together words that inspire you along with their meaning. Use words that will have enough emotional intensity so that you can feel the feeling when affirming.

Affirmation cards - Affirmation cards are a massive reminder to me that everything is going to be OK and to stop the negative self-talk. Not only do they help to pull me out of a funk, but they also inspire and instil a sense of hope. I find them incredibly motivational. These cards can be used at any time when you feel discouraged or when you feel like you need motivation to carry on. You can place them anywhere you will be able to easily access them.

Examples - Some of the examples of the affirmations you may use are; prosperity is mine and I choose to have it. Wealth flows to me easy and abundantly. My life is prosperous. I always make the right decisions. Every day in every way, things are getting better and better. I am strong, fit and healthy, etc.

Incantations are like supercharged affirmations. When saying an incantation, the trick is to get in tune with the emotional charge of what you are saying.

The trick is to say it with intensity and conviction and as though you believe it as much as you believe that the sun will rise tomorrow. Embody what you are saying. If you are affirming that you have the courage to achieve all your goals, stand like you have the courage, breathe like you have the courage, experience your muscle tension like you have the courage. Get into a peak state - be what you are saying!

By embodying the physical state of what you are saying, you begin to train your central nervous system in the state of the incantation - it makes it real to your mind, by 'speaking its language'. It becomes easier and more natural for you to feel courageous, for instance.

Affirmations work solely on the level of the conscious mind and by adding the emotional state to turn your affirmations into incantations, the subconscious mind becomes involved too. Your unconscious mind drives behaviours, so working directly with the subconscious is a great way to get fantastic results and fast.

Chapter Thirteen
Have an Attitude of Gratitude

"When I started counting my blessings, my whole life turned around." - Willie Nelson

Gratitude is a feeling of being thankful and appreciative. As we go through our daily motions and replacing the old with the new, it is easy to fall into the trap of focusing on the negative things in life while taking the good ones for granted.

Successful people practice gratitude. After all, I do not see how you can be called successful if you are not happy and thankful for what life has to offer.

If you stop for a couple of minutes each day to take note of a couple of things you really appreciate in your life, then you will begin to treasure these things. This keeps you focused on the positive aspects of your life and puts you on the road to being happier, healthier and more optimistic. Say thank you in advance, for what is already yours in future. A thankful heart is a happy heart.

As Rhonda Byrne, author of The Secret and Magic said, "Thank you is the bridge from where you are now to the life of your dreams. Your life will change by practising gratitude and saying thank you".

You must count your blessings. When you are grateful for the things you have, no matter how small they may be you will see those things instantly increase in your experience. You will be happier when you count your blessings. The more grateful you are, the happier you will become.

"There is no happier person than a truly thankful, content person." - Joyce Meyer

Some of the benefits of gratitude is that it helps you get your priorities straight. When you keep a list of things to be thankful of it helps you figure out what it is that really matters to you and what you should be spending your energy and your time on. It also helps you to be more optimistic in life. Being more optimistic and happier can have several health benefits such as less stress, better sleep patterns, a healthier immune system, more energy and focus.

When writing about what you are thankful for try to think of how different it would be like if you had to live without the things that you claim to be grateful for. You may even be grateful for witnessing acts of kindness done by other people. It is not a problem to also focus on the challenges and appreciating them because some of those could have brought with them some good lessons to learn from.

Some of the benefits of heart-felt gratitude are that:
- It reduces depression,
- Improves our self-esteem,
- Increases our energy,
- Lowers blood pressure,
- Increases positive emotions such as love and empathy,
- Reduces negative emotions such as envy, hatred and anger,

- Improves job performance.

Should you be seeking guidance into putting to practice gratitude, below are some few ways on how to do so:

- ✓ Think about three people in your life (living or deceased) who have made a difference in your life. Think about them and how grateful you are for how they have positively influenced your life.
- ✓ Make a habit out of sending encouraging texts to someone thanking him or her for what they have done for you.
- ✓ Write it down. Keep a gratitude journal and be specific about what you are thankful for. Try this for 30 days. Please note that it is very important that you write down at least three to four times in your journal.
- ✓ Make a habit of being thankful for big and small things or small acts.

Gratitude is the greatest tool in cultivating the use of elevated emotions or changing from one state of emotion to the other. Using gratitude can change you from survival emotions directly into elevated or creative emotions because it is impossible to be sad and grateful at the same time.

If you could not keep up with practising most of the techniques discussed in this book this is perhaps one technique you ought to be able to practice with the utmost ease, as it does not require any special preparatory steps. You may give gratitude when you wake up or when brushing your teeth, eating a meal, driving, or buying groceries, the list is endless.

The question that often arise from people I have interacted with is, "what do I do when things don't go my way or when they go horribly wrong?" To help with this I have a certain saying that I have adopted by Louis Hay, and you are welcome to say this to yourself too. "All is well, all is well, everything is working out for my highest good, out of this, only good will come and I am safe." This, believe me has a way of calming whatever turmoil you might be dealing with internally.

Chapter Fourteen
Press On, Never Give Up

"Our greatest weakness lies in giving up. The most certain way to succeed is always to try just one more time." - Thomas A. Adison

The words persistence and perseverance have similar meanings when it comes to success and some people use them interchangeably, but they do not entirely refer to the same things. Persistence is the choice to continue to do something, despite difficulty, opposition and struggle hindering you along the way from achieving the goal. The single-mindedness of a person brings out the dedication that he or she wants and needs in order to achieve their dream.

Perseverance on the other hand is the continuation of commitment through action despite the lack of success. It is also the ability to overcome the repetitiveness of problems from difficult situations. Perseverance is more important than just plain persistence, because it is about having stamina and endurance during the time of struggle.

While persistence is a choice, perseverance means surviving the toughest conditions and coming out better on the other side. When it comes to work, perseverance is the hard work you do after you get tired of doing the hard work you already did.

Success does not happen overnight. Successful people in the world today have endured challenges, errors, failures and obstacles. Even if it took them days, weeks, months, years or even decades to fulfil their dreams and goals. If you respect the journey, then you have to respect the work that goes with it.

One of the reasons for the necessity of having these character traits is that as you try to live the life of your dreams, regardless of the goals or ideals you have. Life is not going to simply give it to you on a silver a platter to enjoy without the resistance that comes with it, no matter how good those plans may be. There are many examples of underdogs or heroes of our time as well as previous times, all who have persisted and persevered, stayed on course and met or even exceeded their expectations.

Galatians 6:9 - "Let us not become weary in doing good, for at the proper time we will reap a harvest if we do not give up."

Calvin Coolidge once said, "Nothing in the world can take the place of persistence. Talent will not; nothing is more common than unsuccessful men with talent. Genius will not; unrewarded genius is almost a proverb. Education will not; the world is full of educated derelicts. Persistence and determination alone are omnipotent. The slogan Press On! Has solved and always will solve the problems of the human race."

Those who can "take it" are abundantly rewarded for their persistence. They always reach the goals they set out to achieve. They know that every failure brings with it an equivalent advantage. "Those who have cultivated the habit of persistence seem to enjoy insurance against failure. No matter how many times they are defeated, they finally arrive up at the top of the ladder," Napoleon Hill, Think and Grow Rich.

There are so many people you may know who succeeded through applying these character qualities and to list a few examples as a source of encouragement when things become tough. I will start with the most common ones in history:

Abraham Lincoln

1833 - He failed terribly in business.

1835 - His only girlfriend, with whom he was supposed to marry, died.

1836 - As a result of this loss, he suffered a nervous breakdown and lost his post office job.

1838 - He was badly defeated in his first election for the post of speaker.

1858 - He lost the nomination to US senate and for the post of vice president.

1860 - He finally achieved success and became the president of the United States of America.

These are just a few rough spots in the life of America's greatest Statesman.

Let us look at more examples:

1. Henry Ford's early businesses failed, and he was broke 5 times before he founded Ford Motor Company.
2. Walt Disney went bankrupt after failing at several businesses. He was even fired from a newspaper for lacking imagination and good ideas.
3. Albert Einstein was thought to be mentally handicapped before changing the face of modern physics and winning the Nobel Prize.

4. It took Thomas Edison 1000 attempts before inventing the light bulb. His teachers kept telling him at a young age of how he was too stupid to learn anything.
5. Lucille Ball was regarded as a failed actress before she won 4 Emmys and the Lifetime Achievement Award from the Kennedy Center Honors.
6. American author Jack London received 600 rejections before his first story was accepted. Now that is some thick skin.
7. Michael Jordan was cut from his high school basketball team for not being good enough J. K Rowling was nearly penniless, severely depressed, divorced, and a single mom, who went to school while writing Harry Potter. Rowling went from needing government assistance to being one of the richest women in the world in a 5-year span through her hard work.
8. Nelson Mandela once said, "After climbing a great mountain, one only finds that there are many more mountains to climb".

It is my hope that the list above will always come in handy when dire situations arise, and you need some motivation to keep on keeping on. It is also important to be conscious of certain traits that people with persistence and perseverance have in common:

- **An All-Consuming Vision** - Persistent people have a goal or vision in mind that motivates and drives them. They are often dreamers and visionaries who see their lives as having a higher purpose than simply earning a living. Their visions are deeply ingrained, and they focus on it constantly with great emotion and energy. They often think of this vision first thing when they wake up and it is the last thing on their mind before they go to bed. Reaching this goal becomes the focal point of their life and they devote a major portion of their energies and time toward reaching it.

Burning Desire - Entrepreneur and motivational speaker Jim Rohn once said, "If you really want to do something, you'll find a way. If you don't, you'll find an excuse".

Persistent people want it bad, bad, and they never look for an excuse or a way out. What keeps highly persistent people going is their powerful level of desire. Florence Nightingale once said, "I attribute my success to this; I never gave or took excuses".

Repeated failures, dead ends and periods when it seems like no progress is being made often come before any major breakthroughs happen. People with perseverance have the inner energy and intensity to keep themselves motivated and going through these tough times.

- **Inner Confidence** - People who overcome the odds and achieve greatly are often described as "marching to the beat of their own drum". They know what they want and are seldomly swayed by the opinion of the masses. Having a highly developed sense of who they are allows the highly persistent to continue without being greatly affected by what others think of them or being understood nor being appreciated by those around them. While that inner confidence is challenged and shaken, it never is destroyed and constantly acts as a source of courage and determination.

- **Highly Developed Habits** - Rohn also once said, "Motivation is what gets you started. Habit is what keeps you going". Highly persistent people know it is very difficult to stay continually motivated, particularly during difficult times and when it appears that no progress is being made. They have come to rely upon their self-discipline and developing habits that they can count on to continue down the path towards their eventual goals. They believe the results of the efforts they make today may not be seen for a long time, but they strongly believe that everything they do will count toward their outcome in the end.

- **Ability to Adjust and Adapt** - Persistent people can adjust and adapt their action plan. They do not stubbornly persist in the face of evidence that their plan is not working, but look for better ways that will increase their chances of success. The highly persistent see their journey as a series of dead ends, detours, and adjustments but have complete faith in that they will reach their destination. They are not tied into their ego and are quickly willing to admit when something is not working. Adding to that notion, they are quick to adapt the ideas of others that have proven to work well.

- **Commitment to Lifelong Learning** - Persistent and perseverant people realise that any goal worth reaching will take time, effort, and the continuous learning of new skills and thinking patterns. They welcome change and new ideas and continue looking for ways they can incorporate these into their lives. Ongoing learning is seen as part of a process through which the highly persistent continually expand the range of tools that they must work with. Naturally curious, persistent types not only see learning to reach their goals more quickly, but they also see self-development as a way of life. Learning and continual growth do not end at a certain age or stage of life but they are the essence of life itself, and therefore, never-ending.

- **Modelling Acting as Mentors and Coaches** - While it may appear that highly persistent people act alone and don't need anyone, most have a carefully selected group of people they admire and emulate. It can be people who are actually involved in their lives as mentors/confidantes, or they can be figures whom they have read about and who have deeply impacted them. You will know who these people are, since persistent people will often quote them. Persistent people usually stand out from their environment and are often misunderstood or ridiculed because they can make those around them feel uncomfortable. Having strongly ingrained models helps persistent people sustain and motivate themselves in an environment that is not always supportive.

You must be like Jacob who wrestled with an Angel and said, "I will not let you go unless you bless me," - Genesis 32:26.

Author's notes & instructions

You have reached the end of the book. THANK YOU! In order to make all the techniques work out for you, you must apply the key principle of persistence. If you are merely going to put this to practice on an occasional basis, I am afraid to be the bearer of bad news, but such will be a waste of your time. Persistent application and daily practice are the keys to success.

- Write down the things you want to see happen in the next 6 months in your life.
- Write down the date you want to see the manifestation.
- Meditation is the window into your future including the spiritual realm where the things you desire are.

Meditation additional notes

Although the meditation practice has ties to many different religious teachings, meditation is less about faith and more about altering consciousness, finding awareness and achieving peace.

These days, with the greater need to reduce stress amidst our busy schedules and demanding lives, meditation is increasing in popularity.

Although there is not a right or wrong way to meditate, it is important to find a practice that meets your needs and complements your personality.

Not all meditation styles are right for everyone. These practices require different skills and mindsets. How do you know which practice is right for you?

"It's what feels comfortable and what you feel encouraged to practice," says Mira Dessy, a meditation author and holistic nutritionist.

Here is a list of nine popular types of meditation practice:

- **Mindfulness meditation** - Is about paying attention to your thoughts as they pass through your mind. You do not judge the thoughts or become involved with them. You simply observe and take note of any patterns. This practice combines concentration with awareness. You may find it helpful to focus on an object or your breath while you observe any bodily sensations, thoughts or feelings. If you have any area of your body that is not feeling well, concentrate and send healing energy to that area. Think about what made you happy in the past so that you can have generate the same feelings of happiness. To have confidence, think about your past achievement/s to invite the feelings of confidence. This type of meditation is good for people who do not have a teacher to guide them, as it can be easily practiced on your own.
- **Spiritual meditation** - Spiritual meditation is used in Eastern religions, such as Hinduism, Daoism and in the Christian faith. This is similar to prayer in that you reflect on the silence around you and seek a deeper connection with your God or universe. Spiritual meditation can be practiced at home or in a place of worship. This practice is beneficial for those who thrive in silence and seek spiritual growth.

- **Focused meditation** - Focused meditation involves concentration using any of the five senses. This practice may be simple in theory but it can be difficult for beginners to hold their focus for longer than a few minutes at first. If your mind does wander, it is important to come back to the practice and refocus. As the name suggests, this practice is ideal for anyone who requires additional focus in their life.
- **Movement meditation** - Although most people think of yoga when they hear movement meditation, this practice may include walking through the woods, garden, qigong and other gentle forms of motion. It is an active form of meditation where the movement guides you. It is good for people who find peace in action and prefer to let their minds wander.
- **Mantra meditation** - Mantra meditation is prominent in many teachings, including Hindu and Buddhist traditions. This type of meditation uses a repetitive sound to clear the mind. It can be a word, phrase or sound, such as the popular "Om" sound. It does not matter if your mantra is spoken loudly or quietly. After chanting the mantra for some time, you will be more alert and in tune with your environment. This allows you to experience deeper levels of awareness.
- **Transcendental meditation** - It is more customizable than mantra meditation. The use of a mantra or series of words that are specific to each practitioner. This practice

is for those who like structure and are serious about maintaining a meditation practice.

- **Progressive relaxation** - Also known as body scan meditation. It is a practice aimed at reducing tension in the body and promotes relaxation. Often times, this form of meditation involves slowly tightening and relaxing one muscle group at a time throughout the body. In some cases, it may also encourage you to imagine a gentle wave flowing through your body to help release any tension. This meditation is often used to relieve stress and unwind before bedtime.

- **Loving-kindness meditation** - Loving-kindness meditation is used to strengthen feelings of compassion, kindness and acceptance toward oneself and others. It typically involves opening the mind to receive love from others and then sending a series of well wishes to loved ones, friends, acquaintances and all living beings. Because this type of meditation is intended to promote compassion and kindness, it may be ideal for those harbouring feelings of anger or resentment.

- **Visualization meditation** - Visualization meditation is a technique focused on enhancing feelings of relaxation, peace, and calmness by visualizing positive scenes or images. With this practice, it is important to imagine the scene vividly and use all five senses to add as much detail as possible. Another form of visualization meditation involves imagining yourself succeeding at specific goals, which are intended to increase focus and motivation.

Many people use visualization meditation to boost their mood, reduce stress levels and promote inner peace.

The bottom line:
Whether you are looking to reduce stress or find spiritual enlightenment, find stillness or a flow through movement, there is a meditation practice for you.

Do not be afraid to step out of your comfort zone and try different types of meditation. It often takes a little trial and error until you find the one that fits.

"Meditation isn't meant to be a forced thing," Dessy says. "If we're forcing it, then it becomes a chore. Gentle, regular practice eventually becomes sustaining, supportive, and enjoyable. Open yourself up to the endless possibilities. There are so many different forms of meditation that if one isn't working or isn't comfortable, just try a new one."

Finally, I would like to leave you with these words. All you can do is all you can do and all you can do is enough. However, make sure you do all you can do. I may not know you and our paths may have not crossed but it is my hope that by reading this book, we have met.

SUGGESTED READINGS

The passion to see greater human growth and humanity realising its potential was the driving force towards the drafting and ultimate release of this book. This has taken so many references from many materials I could lay my eyes on that related to each subject matter, and also through the actual personal encounter and realisation of most of these principles and hence, my conviction that following these will surely make one's life a success.

For a long time I had thought success was such an elusive reality and reserved for some until this in depth research on personal success. It is my wish that this makes all your dreams a reality and that your change in this world becomes evident.

In no particular order, below are mentions of some of the material I was able to lay my hands on for references in this book. Feel free to refer to any of them if necessary:

- The Power of Positive Thinking, by Norman Vincent Peale
- See you at the Top, by Zig Ziglar
- Essentiallifeskills.net
- Think and Grow Rich, by Napoleon Hill
- The Power of your Subconscious Mind, by Joseph Murphy
- Mind Power, by John Kehoe
- The Secret, by Rhonda Byrne
- The Magic of Thinking Big, by David Schwartz

- Awakened Imagination, by Neville Goddard
- The Power of awareness, by Neville Goddard
- Your erroneous zone, by Dr Wayne W Dyer
- Becoming Supernatural, Dr Joe Dispenza
- The Power of Purpose, by Les Brown
- Unlimited Power, by Tony Brown
- The Power of Vision, by Dr Myles Munroe
- Men's Search for meaning, by Victor Frankl
- As a man thinketh, by John Allen

About The Author

Dingaan Rahlapane is a certified Life Coach and Strategist by profession. Mentored by the best in the game in the motivational speaking and coaching business, Leb Brown, Tony Robbins and Dean Graziosi. He has been practising as a life coach for the past three years and has incredible record of accomplishment with his clients experiencing and living lives of their dreams.

He offers life-transforming training to students in the field of personal development through the Success Mindset Training course of three weeks. The aim of these sessions is to help clients seeking prosperity and success to regain a sense of focus and direction whilst obtaining the ability to control and direct their minds through proven tools and techniques. Success Mindset is not only about motivation but also discipline and practice for achieving breakthrough in success and unleashing your inner potential and power through tools and techniques he has mastered over the years of serving clients. Dingaan vigorously seeks to help people create lasting change in their lives.

He further ventures into the Ultimate Destiny course for those individuals yearning for a deeper understanding and meaning to life. These sessions help to create a sense of purpose in ones life by clarifying your visions and goals. He also extends his hand to those seeking a mentor as a helping hand towards a new transformation and life experience by being their personal life coach.

www.dingaanrahlapane.co.za

Copyrights

RESET YOUR MINDSET FOR SUCCESS. Copyright © 2021 by Dingaan Rahlapane. All rights reserved. No part of this text may be reproduced, transmitted, decompiled, reverse engineered and retrieval system, in any form or by any means, whether electronic or mechanical, now known or hereinafter invented, without the express written permission of Dingaan Rahlapane and the Publishers.

ISBN | 978-0-639-90151-0

answers consultation publishers

www.answersconsultation.com

www.ingramcontent.com/pod-product-compliance
Lightning Source LLC
Chambersburg PA
CBHW070200100426
42743CB00013B/2989